Revelations of The Metatron

Anonymous

Preface by John Rossner, Ph.D.

1999
Galde Press, Inc.
Lakeville, Minnesota, U.S.A.

First Edition,1995
Second Printing, 1999

Library of Congress Cataloging-in-Publication Data

Revelations of The Metatron / Anonymous.—1st ed.
        p.   cm.
    Diary written by Gary Sornson and translations by Sornson,
wife Lea, and Miguel Sanchez.
    ISBN 1–880090–21–X
    1. Bible.   O.T.   Genesis—Miscellanea.   2. Deluge—Miscellanea.
3. Sacred space—South America—Miscellanea.   4. South America—
—Antiquities—Miscellanea.   5. Sornson, Gary—Diaries.
I. Sornson, Gary.
BF1999.R444   1995
001.9'4—dc20   95–15369
                                                      CIP

Galde Press, Inc.
PO Box 460
Lakeville, Minnesota 55044–0460

Contents

Preface

This is an altogether fascinating book. The Foreword, the Introduction, and the Diary of Gary Sornson read like a thriller. It is a classic adventure story of the discovery of ancient hidden treasure, golden artifacts and an inscription in arcane hieroglyphics in a lost cave in the jungle and mountains of South America.

The deciphering of the mysterious cave inscriptions yield the text of *The Revelations of The Metatron*, purporting to be an ancient cosmic prehistory of the earth and its inhabitants—gods, angels and men—as recorded or inspired by the legendary "Angel of the Presence," or "The Metatron."

The Metatron is the celestial "Adam Kadmon," a pre-existent Cosmic Man or "Son of Man," figure seen by Enoch, Ezekiel, Daniel and other Hebrew prophets and later Kabbalists, during their "Heavenly Journeys" and Visions at the "Throne of God."

Those who have enjoyed reading 19th and 20th Century archetypal accounts of human origins, whether in Helena Blavatsky's descriptions of the seven "root races," or Edgar Cayce's "life readings" concerning the rise and fall of Atlantis, or Zecharia Sitchin's saga of the "struggle between the gods and men" will be fascinated by this book. It is all here: Mesopotamia, Atlantis, Egypt, the Pyramids, Greece, ancient South America, Enoch, Noah, the Flood, tied together in a most interesting fashion, the story of a primordial cosmic battle between powers of Light and Darkness…"on earth and in heaven."

An enhanced version of the Biblical drama unfolds, narrating: the creation of the Heavens; the subsequent fall of rebellious angels; the

ensuing struggle between forces of light and darkness, in heaven and
on earth; the subsequent loss of the paradisial state of existence by
fallen angels or gods; their corruption of early humankind by entering
into sexual union with the "daughters of men;" the production of
hybrid "Nephalim" and "Refalim"—who with their human minions,
"the sons and daughters of Bael," —and their superior powers of
intellect, science and technology—lorded it over and enslaved the
ordinary children of men.

This is followed by and intertwined with the story of a series of
attempted "rescue missions" of the fallen planet by "The Metatron"
and "the Angels of Light," who preside over the higher worlds of
spirit and space.

This results ultimately in the banishment of the fallen angels or
evil gods and their hybrid offspring—the Nephalim and Refalim—
from the surface of the earth back into the lower regions of the heavens, or "fallen space-worlds."

All of this is reminiscent of a number of ancient Enochian and
early Christian Gnostic texts which described the "archons" as "fallen
rulers of some of the planets," or evil "powers of the air," who try to
wreak havoc on the "children of men," who must be rescued from
their grip by the Celestial Representative of the Lord Most High, (who
is "The Metatron," a pre-existent celestial divine-and-human Christ
figure) and the Higher Powers, or Angels of Light.

The work combines elements of futuristic technology with a mis-
used super-psychic and spiritual power by some fallen angels and
most human beings. Like various Enochian, Biblical, and later Kabbal-
istic texts it implies that the corruption of human civilizations, and the
distortion of nature itself, has occurred over and over again through
the interference of fallen powers, influences, and intelligences working
on life forms and within those human souls who act often with superior force and success in the world as "the children of 'Belial."

On the other hand, for those "walking in the Light," this saga
declares like the Bible itself that the "Final Victory" is secure in the
"Plan of the Lord Most High"…who presides over a meaningful (and
originally good) Creation which will one day be restored and trans-
formed into "A New Heaven and a New Earth."

But what about the manuscript itself? Was there really a fantastic
discovery of an ancient text in a golden pyramid in a secret cave in a
remote location in South America?! What do you think? Skeptics and
academics require reasonable evidence.

Could this really be the record of some ancient prophet or scribe's impression of "the words of The Metatron," as in the case of the ancient books of Enoch, or the Apocalypse of John? ... or, is this more simply put, inspired modern fiction?

At this point, we must ask: "Can we answer such questions on the basis of the text alone?" And in the absence of presented proof, no final claims can be made.

Yet, for many this fact will not detract one iota from their fascination with the story itself, which, like the Mahabharata Upanishad in ancient India is set as a classic tale of the Creation and of the subsequent cosmic warfare of "gods and men" concerning issues of "Light and Darkness" in a remote cosmic "pre-history" beyond all verification by ordinary human empirical means.

—by John Rossner, Ph.D. D.Sc. D.Litt.
Professor of Comparative Religion and Culture
Concordia University, Montreal
& President, International Institute
of Integral Human Sciences

Foreword

I have absolutely no proof of the authenticity of what I am about to present to you. All I have are the writings that were given to me. I am sharing how I received them and the pages that were handed to me.

I wish to remain anonymous because I do not want to go through the tortuous questioning and derisive remarks that are sure to follow any statement proclaiming that what I am about to disclose to you may be truly factual.

Those who want to believe will believe anyhow. Those who are the critics are sure to ridicule and condemn.

I do not wish to be subjected to the derision of scoffers or to have my family or friends harassed for something about which they know nothing.

As a result of what I have stated, some of the names and some of the locations have been changed or deleted.

The unbelievable find of hieroglyphic writings on golden columns discovered in a pyramid of gold within a South American mountain is in itself enough to desire anonymity, although I haven't the faintest idea where the pyramid is located.

As a final statement, I cannot say that the reading of the translation of the pre-biblical hieroglyphics about God and all before has not changed my outlook on life, but I have not turned into a crusader.

Now I realize that all Souls have problems and only they can change.

—GAR

Introduction

I 'm not sure if I was Per Sornson's best friend, but just before he left for South America I believe I was his strongest confidant.

In the spring of 1983, Per Sornson telephoned me at my public relations office in New York. As I picked up the phone, I heard the telephone recorder click on.

I had started taping conversations when I was a Vice President of Public Relations with my former company. Many times the president would come back from lunch half drunk and call me to do something. The next day he would forget what he had proposed and raise hell with me for doing something he had told me to do.

That is when I began using my phone recorder. I would play the tape back to myself taking copious notes and meet with the president the next morning when he was sober. By going over my notes he could confirm, deny or change what he had said. That's how I stayed at my job until the president was fired and I was offered a generous early retirement.

That's when I started my own firm and continued my recordings with my clients. Even though I knew it was probably illegal, it saved a lot of grief. But nobody ever questioned me, they just thought I had a great mind.

This time it was Per Sornson.

"Gar, I want you to do something for me that is vitally important." That was Per Sornson's only greeting. "I have some ancient writings that are like nothing ever known. I'm going to South America tomorrow and I want to leave them with you. If I don't come back in a couple of years I want you to publish them."

It had been the previous fall that I had last seen Per. Then it was to help him move into a huge, old, run down early nineteen-hundreds house of clapboard, with the high roof, gingerbread gables and the wide wooden stairs running up to the pillared open porch. It had been left to him by his recently deceased parents who had for years been professors at a local university.

He was splitting from his wife and teenage children. The scene at the move I thought was somewhat ludicrous.

Per had parked a small, beat-up U-Haul truck near the stone steps of the huge stone and stucco English tudor mansion that he had lived in. The home had been given to his wife, along with incredible wealth, by her now demised bachelor uncle.

Per, his teenage son, Mark, and the handy man had begun to carry out small items into the truck. Per looked quite disheveled compared to his always well dressed look in the city. He had grown a shaggy beard and mustache, which, along with his formerly reddish brown hair, was liberally sprinkled with white. He was in a jump suit, which hung loosely on his six-foot-four frame. His face was haggard with sunken eyes. The pupils of his unique light steel blue eyes still sparkled as they always had. His eyes were so startling that they attracted attention wherever he went. He had said his father's family all had the same eyes.

Carrying his clothes, typewriter and little odds and ends was no problem, but moving his walnut desk and two steamer trunks at both ends of the trip was backbreaking. I would have gladly paid a mover to do my job. When he was packed, he spoke to his son and daughter and then his wife Tassy, each in private. When he turned to leave, Tassy said something like "I hope you find what you're looking for, Per. I'll send on the divorce papers."

The way she said it, I suddenly fathomed that this move was not his wife Tassy's idea. I had first met Per Sornson at an American Management seminar in New York City several years ago. We sat next to each other in the class and ate lunch together at noon. Per had received an MBA from Harvard, where he had met his wife Tassy. She was also getting her MBA, which she used later to run her family's extensive investments.

I had gone to Columbia for a degree in journalism where I had met my wife Karen, who went to art school. As is the case of people who do work in New York City, our wives never met. Yet Per and I met for lunch at least once a month. Per was younger than I, but he had made Vice President of Planning for his firm that was listed on the stock exchange.

I helped Per get a management book published that sold well in his company but not much anywhere else. But, as a result of that, when I started my own public relations office I did a lot of work for his firm.

Just before his breakup with his family and his move, Per had quit his job. After his move I had tried to contact Per but he had an unlisted phone. When I made any effort to go to his house he was never there. Though Per lived in a different state he was only a half-hour away.

Now I learned that Per was going to South America.

"Can I meet you at Grand Central Station tomorrow about 4 P.M.?" he asked. "I want to give you these writings."

"It's fine with me," I agreed.

"See you by the center information booth on the upper level at about 4 P.M. Wait for me if my train is late. It's important."

"See you then."

I want you to know, that if what happened when I met Per were an illusion, at the time I didn't think so. I still remember the event vividly and I recall it often.

I was waiting by the upper information booth at the center of the immense pedestrian mall of the cavern-like Grand Central Rail Station. Per Sornson came down the slight ramp from the west that led into the waiting room and then on to 42nd Street. I wasn't expecting him to come that way because the commuter trains arrived on the other side of the station.

Per was immediately conspicuous, but it took a moment for me to identify him. He stopped for just a moment under the high arched entrance leading to the gigantic room where I was. He was dressed from tip to toe in pure white. His suit, shirt, tie and shoes were white. With his now fully white beard, mustache and hair and his height of six feet four, he stood out like he was on stage. Even at a distance I saw his penetrating steel, light blue eyes. Even his carrying cases were white. The brown, wrapped package under his right arm was the only contrast.

I wasn't intending to tape our meeting but when I recognized him I flipped my hidden pocket recorder on.

Just as we started toward each other, for some reason I glanced up because I thought I saw an arc of light.

One of the gigantic carved stone figurines that are placed about the upper rim of the nearly seventy-five foot ceiling of Grand Central broke loose and was falling directly down toward Per.

I yelled,"Look out!"

And without thought I rushed toward him and with my finest high school linebacker tackle, I carried Per sprawling back into the entrance tunnel.

There was a small crash behind us.

When we arose to look, there were the remains of a white porcelain vase and a red rose that had shattered on the floor.

"What the hell was that?" I exclaimed. "I swear I saw one of those huge cement sculptured figurines fall from the ceiling."

"Just Satan's way of saying hello." Per said shakily but seemingly trying to be humorous.

"What do you mean by that?" I asked a little testily.

"When you read what's in this package you'll understand," Per said mysteriously and handed me the brown wrapped package.

Suddenly there were people all around us. Some thanking me for warning them of the falling vase. Others wanting to help us. I heard some say they thought we were fighting. It was all on the tape.

Finally, it was all settled down and the crowds once again surged into the Grand Central mall.

"I have to leave," Per finally commented. "I have to catch a plane to California and then go with my Cousin Lyn to South America. If I'm not back in two years, try to publish or get published what's in that package. We'll split it if I come back. If not, give my half to charity. I have to go catch a taxi."

He turned quickly and headed toward and up the wide marble stairs to the exit where the taxi stands were.

I yelled after him,"Take care of yourself."

He waved without turning around and disappeared.

I went into the waiting room to recover my stability after the falling idol incident and sending Per off.

I decided to go home. I found a seat on the commuter train and discouraged anyone to sit with me. I wanted privacy to read the contents of the package. Actually there were three separate packages tied together. The thinner manila envelope that was on the top had my name and address scripted on it in Per's meticulous handwriting.

There were enough stamps on it to mail the whole package. I guess he figured if he missed me he'd have to mail it.

My hands were shaking when I opened the first envelope.

It read:

Gar, I presume you have noticed my behavior has been somewhat eccentric for the past year. I hope this letter and that which is enclosed will explain some of my actions.

It actually started a couple of years ago. I wish I could explain exactly how it was.

When it began I don't believe I was either awake or asleep.

It was if the phone rang and I was answering it. But instead of just words the vision of my cousin Lyn enveloped me like a warm mist. She spoke to me as it far away but her vaporous form was there.

"Per, it's Lyn."

I knew It was Lyn. For several years, as my life had sped along, her apparition had flashed through my thoughts like caution lights on multiple street corners. There never was any clear image like a positive red or green. She would appear like an unclear specter at all times of day and night, and on unusual occasions.

My cousin Lyn had mysteriously dropped out of sight some years ago and could not be traced. She had signed a divorce decree from her husband and abandoned her children and disappeared with some repulsive looking Mexican man who was crippled in one arm and leg. When last heard from she had telephoned her family and told them she was going on an adventure and would not be able to communicate with them. And she didn't.

Still, I felt her presence in my mind. At any time or place I would receive a fuzzy picture of her standing statuesquely before me with a tanned face and her long, auburn hair. Her countenance looked as it had when we were young and in love. We had spent a summer together traveling Europe with my Uncle Gary and Aunt Lea, and we fell in love when we were both eighteen. But we separated and went to college. We knew we could not marry because we were cousins, so we married others.

But now that she had disappeared, the thoughts of her became stronger until I could think of little else.

I told Tassy and she was furious. That's when I finally moved out.

One night last fall I was sleeping and having an unusually vivid dream of Lyn, when I heard my phone ring.

When I picked up the receiver I heard, "Per, it's your cousin Lyn. I got your number from Tassy. She wasn't very civil."

I realized immediately that this was for real. My mind cleared and focused. I believe I remember almost everything we said. It went something like this:

"Lyn, where the devil are you?"

"I hope I'm not with him."

"Who?"

"The devil."

"That's an odd thing to say."

"Not if you'd been through what I've been through the last few years."

"Are you on drugs?" I blurted out. For I had often fantasized why she had disappeared.

That seemed to take her by surprise because she paused.

"No," she said softly. "But my life has been as if I were filled with mushrooms."

I felt relieved but curious.

"Where have you been? I've had everyone searching for you everywhere." I lied because I had no idea where to look for her. I was both happy to hear from her and angry I had not heard from her before.

"Did you ever read my father's diary and the translations that were in the package he gave you at your wedding? He said he gave them to you. But I know his mind was a little blurred from drinking."

Suddenly I remembered the package my Uncle Gary had given to me on my wedding day.

He had come to me the day before my wedding. He had seemed to be quite sober. He had handed me an oilskin wrapped parcel. He had told me that it wasn't a wedding present but it was to keep until after his death. Lyn was to also receive a similar packet. If, for any reason, Lyn was not around to inherit it, I should take care of what was inside and present it to the world. When he died, I simply forgot about it. I had forgotten where I had put it anyhow.

My Uncle Gary had not always been a drinker. When I was young he had been my idol. He was a world traveler, international executive for his firm, and an inventor. He spoke several languages. He had been awarded a couple of honorary doctorates.

I think my father and mother, who were college professors, both resented his receiving these awards because they had gotten their Ph.D.s the hard way with long, tough hours of study. But they never mentioned it.

It was after the plane crash in South America, when he and my Aunt Lea were returning to bury my cousin, Scott, who had been killed in a freak lightning accident. Their plane had also been struck by lightning and their pilot had been seriously injured. My uncle became a despondent man. And when my Aunt Lea was killed in another freak accident by electricity in a bathtub, he delved even deeper into alcohol. I never realized how really traumatic this all was until I read the papers that were in the oilskin package and the reason he worried about Lyn. Of course he could have had concerns for my safety, too—which he didn't seem to worry too much about because he entrusted me with the package.

And, Gar, I hate to put you in this tenuous position.

I now wondered what I had gotten myself into without even knowing it. I recalled the incident at Grand Central Station. I immediately remembered vividly the flash of light just before I thought I saw the concrete statue hurtling toward Per. I certainly didn't want to be a martyr for something I knew nothing about. I was eager to get through with the reading and find what was in the other packages. I continued to read Per's letter.

Anyhow, Gar, when I was distracted into thinking about the package my Uncle Gary had given me, I was not able to recall everything that Lyn said. But I do remember her saying, "Since you are not with Tassy anymore, I would like you to come to South America with me. I'm coming with Miguel Sanchez to California next spring and you can come back with me."

I recall asking where she was.

"I'm in South America. For security, I won't tell you where."

"You're calling from South America?"

"Yes, didn't you know."

"No. Who is this Sanchez guy? And what are you doing down there?"

"When you read my father's diary you'll know. It's in the package. But right now I have to go. I'm going back into the mountains at dawn. I hope you can come back with me next spring."

Suddenly there was a buzzing of static on the phone and it went dead. I waited but no other call came through. I have to admit I was very frustrated.

The next day after searching I found the oilskin parcel at the bottom of one of my steamer trunks. The reading of my uncle's diary and The Revelations was extremely fascinating. I'm sure you'll find it to be too.

Anyway, Gar, my cousin Lyn did call a few days ago. She wants me to publish the diary and the Revelations. And of course I thought of you.

Also, the reason Lyn is in South America is that Miguel Sanchez found a new cave next to the one my Uncle Gary and Aunt Lea discovered with him years ago where the hieroglyphics were uncovered. She is helping him decipher new hieroglyphics in the new cave. When it is completed they want to announce the discovery to the world.

The new hieroglyphics are supposedly those of The Metatron who also wrote the Revelations. According to the new hieroglyphics he was also the white man god that appeared and lived with the many Indian tribes of South, Central and North America. The white man god that was variously identified as Quetzalcoatl, Kukulan, Virocacaha and many other names.[1]

As you will discover in the writings in the other packages, The Metatron is supposedly the first Angel and the Scribe of God who was incarnated on earth to help those survivors of the great floods on this part of the then separated earth. The Metatron traveled to the Indian tribes to teach and train them in building, in food production and how to irrigate, to worship and study and use of the heavens.[2]

But, Lyn says the translation from the new cave shows that the fallen Archangel Belzebub came to Central America and was viewed as a plumed serpent and also called himself Quetzalcoatl. Belzebub tried to discredit the works of The Metatron by teaching war, teaching ideas that failed the food systems and teaching worship of himself and the heavens.[3]

Lyn and Sanchez want you to somehow publish those translations I have given you. When we return they will announce the new writings of The Metatron.

Gar, I guess this is what my life is all about, and what I've always dreamed of, being involved in something that reveals something extraordinary to all mankind.

I may have told you that my father's and Lyn's father's two older sisters were much into the psychical and metaphysical fields. Before they died in World War II, they told our families that they believed that Lyn's father and mother were destined to do something that was extremely important in their lifetime. They also foretold that Lyn and I would together do remarkable things together. My aunts believed in past lives—though I don't believe I do—and they felt all of us were from a superior past.

Anyway, Gar, please find a way to publish the accounts I have left with you. If possible, do it before we return—if we do.

Ever Your Friend,
Per Sornson

1. Notes can be found on page 199.

Per Sornson's letter and the events at Grand Central Station spurred me on to read what was in the package he had left for me. It was a Friday night and I had anticipated some interference from my reading. But it wasn't so. My wife, Karen, was behind in designing the cover for a new book and the publisher was pushing her for a Monday deadline. I told her I had a strange meeting with Per but I could tell that she wasn't listening. So, after a fast soup and sandwich, I was able to closet myself in my little study and read of the discovery of the caves and the Revelations of The Metatron.

My mind was reeling when I finally crawled in bed about two Saturday morning. Karen was still painting.

Saturday and Sunday I twice re-read Lyn's father's diary and the Revelations—which were much different than that of the Bible. Sunday evening I received a phone call from Per. I put the tape on.

"Gar, it is Per."

"Where are you?"

"California with my cousin Lyn and Miguel Sanchez. Did you read the writings?"

"Three times."

"What do you think?"

"Per, are these really true?"

Per didn't answer immediately. Then he said, "I hadn't even thought about them being anything but factual. Here, you talk to Lyn."

There was a pause, and I could hear a discussion going on in the background, although I couldn't make out what was being said. Then, "Gar, this is Lyn, Per's cousin. It's nice to meet you even by phone. Per has talked about you in glowing terms all day."

That was nice to hear since the relationship between Per and myself had always seemed to be driven more by me than Per.

Lyn continued, "Per says that you are in publishing."

"Public relations is my field. I sometimes put small booklets and pamphlets together."

"But you do know publishers?" she said in a questioning manner.

"Mostly the staffs of the publishers," I explained.

"You know Mrs. Wallace, who is the principal owner of a publishing company?" she again asked a question.

"Well, yes, I've done some work for her personally and I've gone to a few functions with her," I acknowledged.

My acquaintance with Mrs. Wallace was one of those New York contact stories. I did publicity for a few charities—mostly because I did it for nearly cost plus a couple of free tickets. It occasionally paid off because of the people I met and got business from.

At one of the dinner functions I met an executive of the publishing firm, who, when he found out I sometimes published small books, wanted his autobiography done. He didn't want to use his staff people to do it. I had always been interested in memoir writing and once even taught an evening adult class in it.

I spent a lot of odd evenings with him and finally put his memoirs together. I thought it was interesting, especially for its inside view of the firm where he worked. But once it was done, the only review was quite placid and it sold only a few hundred copies. But the executive was happy.

He called me one afternoon and said he had an extra ticket to a dinner that night at some award function in New York. If I could go I would be sitting at the Mrs. Wallace's table.

Of course I went.

I was in an expansive mood that night and my conversation was the highlight of the table. I made a big impression on Mrs. Wallace. When they found that I did charity publicity, Mrs. Wallace asked if I could do the publicity for a charity she had coming up and of which she was the chairwoman.

We worked hard together, with others, on it and the event was highly successful. I also did a couple of other charities of which she was on the boards.

She got me a lot of work that paid some good money. And my wife and I went to a lot of functions with Mrs. Wallace. So I had to say to Per's Cousin Lyn that I knew Mrs. Wallace.

Lyn then asked, "If I sent you some proof of the pyramid and the hieroglyphics do you think Mrs. Wallace would look at them?"

"I suppose she might. Lyn, is this all true?"

"I've been there. It's fabulous," she stated emphatically. "It's even more. The golden pyramid is also therapeutic. Miguel's disfigurement from his plane accident has practically been cured. We both have grown over an inch in the few years we've been there. The food we bring into the pyramid never spoils. And the sunlight coming into the pyramid that shines on the golden walls keeps me lightly tanned.

"But that's not why we're calling. We want to send you a box with additional proof of the hieroglyphics.

"When we get back to the pyramid we'll send you photographs and all sorts of things. If we can.

"And we'll send you some of the translations of the new writings. They tell of The Metatron's travels throughout the Americas who many of the many ancient Indian tribes refer to as the bearded white man god, who was variously known as Quetzalcoatl, Kukulcan, Viracocaha and many others—including Omac who led my parents to the caves in the mountains.

"We want you to publish my father's diary and my mother's notes and of course the Revelations of The Metatron—or to get them published.

"Per, I and Sanchez are leaving tomorrow for the caves in South America. We'll send you a steel box full of things you'll need to prove the golden pyramid is real.

"I've been going on long enough, Gar. I'll take care of Per."

From the way she sounded, I had a feeling Lyn was happy to be with Per.

"Gar, it's Per. It's true Lyn really looks fantastic and Sanchez looks in good health for his age.

"Gar, the package with the steel box should arrive Tuesday. We're sending it by special messenger to your office."

"Steel box?" I asked the question.

"Yes, it will be sealed inside to keep everything intact. Open it carefully. Gar, do you have any questions?"

"Yes, where are you going?" I was really curious.

"To South America."

"Where in South America?" I pressed him for an answer.

"Even I don't know. Lyn won't tell me until we get there."

I figured I wasn't going to find out. "OK. Be careful. Good luck and let me hear from you."

"I will. "

I sat for a few moments mulling over our conversation. Then I rewound the long play tape on the answering machine and listened to the conversation again.

I sweated it out Tuesday waiting for the messenger. The package arrived late Thursday afternoon in an oversized leather briefcase that was discretely handcuffed to a short, stocky woman in her thirties.

I showed her my I.D., signed her forms and received the briefcase.

Inside the briefcase was the metal container. Inside that were the materials sealed in plastic and underneath that was wrapped in waxed paper. What was in the box was not so extensive as I had expected. There were a few sketches of the caves but no diagram or map of how to get there.

There were a few typed pages signed by Lyn explaining the caves, the golden pyramid and the new caves with hieroglyphics carved in marble-like stones. The new hieroglyphics told of The Metatron's travels and his teaching the Indians. Also his anger at Belzebub who came to destroy his work. And finally his return to the golden caves to stay and record his time on Earth.

There were two weathered pages of hieroglyphics and what I assumed were Spanish translations. There were copies of Lyn's father's diary in his original writing that had been Xeroxed. Finally, there were a few pages of Lyn's mother's notes relating to the caves and the arguments over the translations and the final agreements. It told how she researched the names of all in the hieroglyphics and used the English versions of the Hebrew-Greek and some obscure sources such as the Amilous.

I had a hard time believing that what was sent was proof of the caves and hieroglyphics.

I did what I said I would do and called Mrs. Wallace.

She was eager to see what I had to show her.

Mrs. Wallace had not been well for some time, but she would make an effort to see me at her office. She said she had not been there for some time and this would be a good excuse.

Perhaps what I had would be something she could leave to the world, she said.

I guess I must have been quite enthusiastic about hieroglyphic Revelations, The Metatron, the golden pyramid and the discovery of who was the legendary bearded white god man of the many American Indian tribes of long ago.

I met with Mrs. Wallace that Friday afternoon. I was ushered into her office before she arrived. The people of the publishing firm were all abuzz at Mrs. Wallace's anticipated arrival. The offices and the hallway around where she would enter were filled with employees as I came into her office.

As she came, there was a great commotion and I could hear greetings and loud murmurs. She was finally escorted through the door by several executives.

I could tell she had spent a great deal of time with her beautician and in choosing the right dress. But underneath I could tell that Mrs. Wallace was a very sick woman.

"Gar, it's good to see you again," she greeted me.

Shortly everyone but she and I were asked to step outside.

I cannot remember precisely how the rest of the conversation went because I failed to turn on my tape recorder. But I explained in limited detail how I received the briefcase and the contents in the steel box which I took out. I told Mrs. Wallace of the conversations with Per and Lyn. I briefed her on what was in the metal container. Mrs. Wallace was very excited.

I set the steel box on her desk and lifted the lid.

At once there was a blue flame and the entire contents of the container was ablaze. A pervasive sulphur odor arose.

For a moment my mind was stunned. But the elderly woman picked up her water container and doused it on the conflagration. At the same time she screamed for help.

I stood still, dazed as two security guards rushed into the room followed by the executives who had led her in before. One of the security men grabbed a small fire extinguisher from behind a plant and expertly sprayed the foam onto the box.

"Take him and get him out of here," Mrs. Wallace shrieked as she pointed at me.

The guards grabbed me.

"Did he try to hurt you?" one of the executives shouted.

"No, but that damn box was set on fire. Throw him and his box out," she commanded. "And don't ever let him in here again."

"Want me to call the police?" someone asked.

"No, just get him out," were the last words Mrs. Wallace ever said to me.

I was rudely ushered to my car with the scarred metal container and its soaked and burned contents, along with the briefcase in which I had put them.

A company guard followed me out to the street. I went to my car and then on to my home still shaking.

I looked into the metal box when I arrived home. All that was left were the fringes of wet, charred pages and it still smelled like sulphur.

At that moment I was convinced that there was a devil.

It also reinforced my belief in the existence of God. For God was now my only hope. Almost at once I felt relief, and a calm drifted over me. I thought of the Revelations of The Metatron and how it tied in directly with Genesis of the Bible and the Pentateuch. At that time I felt everything that Lyn assured me was true about the hieroglyphics was in fact true.

I did not discuss with my wife the events that had happened.

I called Mrs. Wallace at her home the next day to try to explain my own amazement at what had happened to the metal box. She told her maid to tell me never to contact her again.

I went to church with the family the Sunday after the disastrous morning. I had always been an intermittent church attendee. I paid my dues and I knew the pastor well. But I never felt I could bring any of my problems to him because of knowing him well.

By Wednesday afternoon I was so shaken that I found a church near my office and found a pastor that would see me. I told him I was in possession of some extremely valuable papers and I felt endangered by one no less than Satan himself. The pastor queried me about them. But I would only reveal they were ancient hieroglyphic translations that revealed things from before the Bible.

He asked if I felt in danger.

I said I did and that twice I had violent accidents while in contact with them.

He began to question me about my past, my church affiliation, my work, family and other more intimate things.

I felt uneasy, excused myself politely and began to leave.

He asked to say a prayer and I agreed.

His prayer was rather disjointed, but he prayed for my soul and my troubles.

I was glad when I had left. I wished I had not gone.

The next day my own pastor called saying he had received a phone call from a minister in Manhattan who related a strange tale. Did I want to see him? To which I politely said no and never spoke to him about it again.

I called Per's ex-wife, Tassy, several times over the next two years to see if she had heard from him. She hadn't. Finally she told me she was getting married again and she didn't want me to call. She said she would contact me if she heard from Per again.

My business went downhill. I got a few charity promotions but few contacts paid off. I got no work from my main clients, and Per's old company gave me no new business. Finally I closed my office in New York.

I have not heard from Per again. Per left no money to publish any of the writings, so I decided to try to find a publisher.

Postscript: At first it appeared that finding a publisher was no trouble. An acquaintance introduced me to an editor for a medium-sized publishing house. The editor thought the diary and hieroglyphics were "earth shattering." I signed a contract. However, the editor informed me that because of the nature of the book it would take a long time to get it to the market.

After a year of phoning and discussing its progress, my calls were interrupted by a continuous busy signal. A few days later I read in the newspaper that the publishing firm was in bankruptcy. I also was not able to contact the editor.

It took another year with the expense of a lawyer to sort out my status with the manuscript. One day it was delivered to my lawyer with the signed contract. No further explanation of any consequence was given.

I languished about for nearly a year before finally sending out a few inquiries to agents I had met or whose names I recognized. No one wanted to take on the project. I finally met an acquaintance at a literary event who had a business life that paralleled my own. I induced him to read the writings. He was extremely enthusiastic about them. He agreed to take on the entire promotion: agent's function and quasi-editor of the manuscript.

He too found problems with editors being fired or quitting their company who expressed interest in the works.

An additional note: In the summer of 1994 a reader of the manuscript told me that an associate of hers, who had also read the writings, informed her that while traveling through South America he had heard a broadcast of a massacre of an Indian tribe by unknown terrorists in a remote mountain village. Included in the atrocity were a white man and woman from the United States. One Indian had escaped and after weeks had made his way to civilization to tell the story. The escaped Indian was returning to the devastated village to bury the dead.

I called Per Sornson's ex-wife, Tassy. She had heard nothing.

But in September Tassy called me. She had received a small letter addressed only to "Mrs. Per Sornson (?), Somewhere in the New York City Area." (The name, of course is changed to protect the living as mentioned in the first pages of this book.) The letter was crumpled and seemingly singed and burned on one edge. The letter was from someone whom Tassy believed was Miguel Sanchez—although the signature was scorched. Though the writing was somewhat strange and irrational, it related the deaths of Per Sornson and his Cousin Lyn. It also told of the destruction of all of the vast work of their translations they had been doing in the caves in the mountains in South America. He did not mention where he was, nor did the envelope reveal the place from where it was sent. He was going back to the village where the killings had occurred. Tassy was amazed that the post office had been able to deliver the letter.

Final note: In the fall of 1994, I was to take a plane trip to visit friends. I decided not to go. The plane I would have taken crashed and all on board were killed. I hope I may continue to remain anonymous.

—GAR

The Diary of Gary Sornson

March 15

(Wife) Lea, and daughter, Lyn, had a birthday party for me tonight. They gave me a watch with every conceivable gadget on it. Tells time in every time zone, has a compass and even a weather forecast.

It's hell to be sixty. But for a few aches and pains, I feel great. I did thirty sit-ups and twenty push-ups along with my usual two mile walk with Lea today. Lea is in great shape—of course she's fifteen years younger than I am.

Son, Scott, couldn't make it as he had two major mid-terms at college tomorrow. He called and wanted me to know he contributed a few dollars for the watch. I'm glad he's doing great at college.

All in all it was a good birthday.

March 21

Some Mexican guy named Miguel Sanchez showed up at my door today. Raunchy looking little character, with strange, steel-blue eyes.

He had two old sheets of manuscript with hieroglyphics and a couple more in Spanish that were supposed to be the translation. He said they were from someplace in South America and were valuable as hell. They were supposedly taken from some chiseled metal tablets in a cave. He was a little vague!

He wants me to finance his two-man expedition to the cave and he'll split anything he finds.

The only thing I did for him was to have the housekeeper, Madge, feed him. He acted as if he hadn't eaten in a week.

He said he didn't have a place to sleep, but I wasn't about to let the shabby creep stay at the house.

March 22

That little bum Miguel Sanchez was back today.

He snuck up behind me as I was weeding in the orchards this morning. I damn near hit him with the shovel I was digging with. He's a repugnant, skinny guy with big warts on his face and a funny looking eye. His hands and face look like he's been in a hundred fights. Looks to be about forty years old, but his face is so scraggly I could be off ten years either way. He is as Mexican dark with straight black hair as I am Icelandic fair with wavy white hair. But strangely his eyes are the same light-pupiled blue as mine—even his weird eye.

He's a persistent SOB. He again wanted to outline his plan. He seems to think the hieroglyphics in the cave are pre-biblical and reveal many things before then.

Sounds intriguing but I think he is a little daft.

I would have listened more to him but Lea called out and wanted me to go shopping with her.

I had my housekeeper, Madge, feed him again. She was furious. She complained he stank like a stable bum. Madge and I don't often agree, but this time I had to admit she was right.

I made a date to sit down with him tomorrow after my exercise and nap. I gave him ten dollars to get a bath and shave. I also gave him some of my old clothes, including underwear and a pair of shoes.

Madge told Lea about Sanchez and she was furious with me for letting the disreputable character come around.

I'm going to fire that old bat, Madge!

I didn't tell either Lea or Madge that I've invited him back tomorrow.

March 23

Miguel Sanchez showed up right on time.

He's eerie!

I was watching for him and suddenly he's there at the door. I don't know how he snuck up without my seeing him.

He looked and smelled better in my clothes, although they hung on him like a gunny sack. I hadn't realized that he was thinner than I am or shorter than my five feet ten. He sure is uglier though.

The shave didn't do his scrubby face any good. His skin is so pock marked and blemished and he has warts all over. With his strange, shifty eye and his dark features and coal black hair, he looks mean. But his voice is soft, though he always seems excited and he has that Mexican accent. At least I guess he's Mexican.

He talked for two hours about his background. He claims he has a Ph.D. from the University of Mexico in both archaeology and languages.

He says he has been on digs in Egypt, Mexico and several South American sites.

He claims he discovered the two pieces of manuscript at someplace in South America—though he won't say where. And he won't let me read them unless I show interest in financing his expedition.

I fed him and kicked him out after a couple of hours. The guy is too weird for me and I told him so.

I also wanted to check out some of his background.

March 24

I called my professor friend in the archaeology department at the University of Mexico. The professor remembered Miguel Sanchez, all right. Sanchez as around to see him a couple of months ago trying to get him to finance his expedition to South America. Sanchez told him that he had gotten his Ph.D. from Stanford in both archeology and languages.

Sanchez had flashed the same two old sheets of manuscript at my friend. But like with me, Sanchez never really showed him anything.

March 25

I called another friend in archeology at the University of Stanford.

He didn't know any Miguel Sanchez even though my friend has been at Stanford for thirty years.

March 26

My Stanford contact called back today and said he found no record of any Miguel Sanchez ever registering in any class at Stanford.

Sanchez is just a con artist—I think.

March 27

Miguel appeared today. Right after my nap, he rang the doorbell.

He was back to his old scruffy ways. My old clothes looked almost as rumpled and dirty on him as those he wore on the first day he came to the house.

He seemed all upset. I don't know why I let him in after I found out what a liar he is.

His excuse was that the local police had found him sleeping in the alley and had hauled him in for vagrancy for a night. Then they took him to the edge of the county and dropped him off. It had taken him eight hours to walk back to my place and keep away from the police.

I kept smelling him for alcohol but that didn't seem to be his problem. I guess that's why the little creep fascinates me. What's his game? Probably just money.

I confronted him with the disclosure of his background by my professor friends.

For the first time he got mad. He ranted and raved about the academic system and college professors and how unfair they were to geniuses like himself.

I became a little frightened.

If I hadn't agreed with him and told him so, I don't know where we would have ended up.

I don't have any regular advanced degrees, but as everyone knows I have honorary doctorate in science and languages myself, because of all my inventions, international achievements and knowledge of twenty six languages and dialects. And I still don't know grammar.

So when I got a word in edgewise and explained all this to him, he calmed down and admitted he had lied about his degrees, but he swore the manuscript was no fake and he was truthful about finding it in a remote village in the mountains of a South American country—though he wouldn't say where. The hieroglyphic tablets are in a cave.

He's so sneaky that when I begin to believe him, he does something that makes me aware he's a liar.

I know he's not telling me everything. I told him to think it over tonight and decide tomorrow if he is going to tell me the true story about the manuscript and the cave. He just clammed up, but I believe he's thinking about it.

I let him sleep in the fruit barn on a folding cot I have out there. I checked the locks on the house and garage doors. Lea would have a fit if she knew he was sleeping on the property. But I don't want him to get picked up on a vagrancy charge again—and maybe my kindness will loosen his tongue a little.

March 28

I was right!

The little sneak Sanchez finally told me the whole story. It's gold! A huge, old, bearded white man revered as a god by the Indians exchanges gold for goods. Each year at Christmas time the natives bring a gold artifact to their Catholic priest from the hidden cave. The priest will take the gold sculptured piece to the city on the plane that comes in occasionally with supplies. He will then buy medicines and other needed items for his Indian parishioners. He goes to a different dealer each time for anonymity.

Miguel spent several years with the Indians and won the confidence of the priest, who gave him the manuscript papers that he copied. He believes the hieroglyphics of his manuscript papers are from some gold objects that are too sacred to be brought out of the cave.

Only the ancient, white, bearded Omac knows where the cave is hidden. Miguel thinks under the right circumstances he can get into the cave. I wondered why he couldn't get there while he was still in the village before. But I thought I would spring that on him after I got more of his story.

March 29

Sanchez began to open up today. The Catholic priest is very interested in finding out about the hieroglyphics in the cave. But he is unable to get anyone to lead him to the cave. No one trusted Sanchez that far either. The real key is that he now wants me to go on the search with him. There is a legend of the arrival of a white man with light blue eyes, totally white hair, a white beard and clothed in white raiment. I don't have a white beard but I certainly fit the rest of the personal description—and I can always wear a white robe. The white man with light blue eyes is to be accompanied by a dark complexioned man also with light blue eyes. And Miguel fits that picture perfectly. It's odd! Maybe another of his con jobs!

He explained that when he first met me, he thought I was perfect for the job as the white man but that I was too old to go on such a strenuous expedition into the mountains and cave. But after seeing me do my workouts he's changed his mind.

Actually I'm very excited. I've traveled all over the world but this looks like something I've never done before.

It's not the gold. We have all the money we'll ever need at our age. Scott and Lyn will inherit enough and they are both smart.

An exploration like this sounds like a fitting way to end up my life. What if there really are pre-biblical writings? The Mayan Indians were supposedly around for thousands of years—and Quetzalcoatl was a legendary white man with a beard—who knows??

Maybe I'll try taking the lying Sanchez' word this time.

I brought Sanchez in from the fruit barn and let him sleep in the guest room in the basement. But I locked the door to the basement. I still don't trust Sanchez that much. I didn't tell wife, Lea.

March 30

I have to admit that Miguel is fascinating. He is as unorthodox as I am.

If he hadn't lied to me so much, I'd feel better about his story of the gold in the cave and the authenticity of his two-page manuscript.

Housekeeper Madge threatened to quit after she found out Sanchez was sleeping in the house. Maybe I'll fire her before she can quit! She's so damned independent. Even though I pay her a fortune, she thinks she is doing us a favor by housekeeping and cooking for us. It's a good thing she lives in her own house and goes home at night. I couldn't stand her otherwise.

March 31

I fired Madge! She said she wouldn't be in the same household with the repugnant Sanchez—even though I'd cleaned him up. So I paid her and told her to get out!

April 1

Madge called Lea about Miguel. Lea really got upset. But we sat down and talked for three hours with both Sanchez and myself.

I finally broke down and told Lea about planning an expedition to South America. I lied to Lea and told her—and Sanchez agreed—that he had a Ph.D. in archeology from the University of Mexico. That made Lea feel better. Lea knows my wanderlust and she understands my desire to explore South America as we've only been there a few times on short trips.

I explained that Sanchez was an expert and he was going to be our guide. Sanchez really opened up and convinced her—and me—that it was the greatest archeological exploration of all time.

Lea was excited with his story and she agreed with the trip and she wants to go. She said she hoped this wasn't an April Fool's joke.

April 2

Lea talked Madge into coming back with the understanding that Madge didn't have to clean Sanchez' room but twice a week and that she could send his clothes to the laundry. I thought it was ridiculous, but I went along with Lea's wishes as we had a lot to do.

We'll be taking off in a few weeks and, as Lea says, Madge is honest and won't run off with all of our household furnishings.

April 3

Sanchez revealed today that he is an expert pilot and that he was the one who had flown the priest in and out of the village with the gold sculptures and brought the supplies back. I hope he is not lying, because he wants to fly an airplane into the mountains where the village and cave is. He doesn't want anyone else to know where we are going.

Damn, this sounds interesting! It's just what I need at my age to quit wasting away. I haven't flown a plane for several years, but I can still co-pilot. And the search sounds fantastic.

April 4

We decided not to tell Lyn or Scott what kind of adventure we are going on. We'll make out it's just a regular trip to South America.

I started to let my beard grow. I hope it comes out white.

(The next few weeks of journal pages tell of the preparation for the trip, the rigors of physical conditioning and the commercial plane trip to South America. It tells of the expensive purchase through a broker of a small private plane in South America because no one wanted to rent them one.

The pages describing the point of take-off and the flight into the mountains are omitted to protect the location of the village and the cave.)

July 13

Arrived at the village after flying several hours into majestic snow-capped mountains. What a pilot! He suddenly dipped the plane into an area that seemed covered with vegetation. He did several unusual maneuvers and then circled. Suddenly the ground cover was opened up as we could see men, women and children carrying back the bushes and even small trees until a runway unfolded. Sanchez came sweeping in and landed on the postage stamp runway.

It was beautiful. The dry dust rose up behind us like the rooster tail of water in the wake of a high speed racing boat. He turned the plane about twenty feet from the runway's end that was still bounded by brush. As we swung around I could see a sharp drop of hundreds of feet a short distance from the wing tip. Sanchez, Lea and I all shouted hurrah as we swept down the landing strip in the opposite direction. As we did, huge pots with the bushes were filled in behind us by those we could now discern as Indians.

Miguel was elated because there was little wind. He says there is almost a constant high wind that sweeps over the mountains. We surely picked the right day to come.

It was when we departed the plane that I got a great surprise. Miguel had told me but I had forgotten.

As we came into land, the village had emptied with the Catholic priest leading the entourage of Indians out to meet us, a splendid sight all dressed in their native finery. When I opened the door to the little plane and stepped out on the wing, there was a great commotion among the Indians and then they all bowed to the ground.

I was dressed in my white linen suit and had cultivated my beard and mustache, which, like my hair, was pure white. Lea told me I looked like a Civil War Southern colonel, but to the Indians I must be like a god.

The Indians are planning a feast for tonight so I am writing this before the whole thing starts. We're quartered in a one-room dirt-floored hut.

July 14

I awoke with a terrible hangover this morning—as did Lea, Sanchez and all of the villagers. The drinks they had were potent.

It's freezing here. The wind came up during the last part of the feast. The bitter, wet cold comes right into the skin. The white wool capes that Sanchez made us bring were certainly welcome. But even our sleeping bags on top of the wool mats were not warm enough. I shivered half the night until Lea came over and crawled in when the fireplace died down.

I learned a couple of things last night. Sanchez was born in the village. He also was the pilot that takes the Catholic priest Juan out to sell the artifacts that Omac gives them when they go to the cities for medicine and crucial supplies.

The priest was also born in the village and is an Indian who went to the lowlands to study. He was given this parish. When he was drunk last night, along with everyone else, he showed us all the collection of artifacts he was going to take to the cities next time. They were worth a small fortune. Most were wood, stone and copper, but a few were gold, and their weight seemed to prove them solid. The gold ones were from the cave.

I think the priest was foolish to show us his collection. I guess he trusts us.

We ate leftovers from last night's feast. All we can do is wait until Omac arrives.

July 15

I am exhausted. I think the high altitude is getting to me. Of course the excitement, the strange food and potent drinks could have a lot to do with it. Also, I am feeling my age. I slept most of the day.

It's very quiet in the village.

The Catholic priest is very excited about Omac coming. He told us he hopes we can find out about the hieroglyphics in the cave. He has heard about them since he was a child. He feels they are something very old.

July 16

It began in the early morning at the dawn, I had slept restlessly because of the greasy tasting meat and strong drink that the Indians might have liked, but I didn't. It didn't seem to bother Lea or the ugly Indian guy, Sanchez, as I could hear them snoring.

I was awakened from my stupor by a commotion and babbling of the Indians. But it was the suddenly absolute silence that made me bolt to my feet. I knew from this sequence of furor and silence that there was probably danger outside. I think it was the eerie, utter silence that awakened wife, Lea, and Sanchez. We all had our guns and knives in our hands when the Indian aide of the priest slipped through the door.

It's lucky he wasn't shot.

"It's Omac, the keeper of the caves. He's here to take you," The aide told us.

I remember I wanted to go the bathroom, but I followed the aide outside, with Lea and Sanchez behind me. There was an eerie cold mist.

There in a semicircle was the entire village facing a seated, huge man in a great poncho and headband flecked with gold and green stones. But it wasn't until he rose that I realized how really big he was. He was enormous. I guessed he was well over eight feet tall. He towered above five-foot-six Indians. As he came toward us the only thing I could think of was a huge, cat-like movement. His entire bodily actions seemed effortless.

Beneath his gold and green stone headband his long hair was as pure white as mine. What surprised me the most was that his skin was even fairer than mine. Sanchez had told me he was a white man, but I had expected Omac to be darker. His skin was almost radiant. He looked as Icelandic as any of my ancestors. Another unexpected thing were his steel blue eyes—the same as mine and Miguel Sanchez.

Omac greeted us in perfect Spanish, his steel blue eyes flashing and his perfect white teeth showed as he smiled slightly.

Omac's appearance was entirely unexpected. I had envisioned a large wizened, wrinkled, toothless old Indian. Omac was a giant. He seemed to stoop a little, but otherwise he seemed in excellent condition.

He spoke to us a little, most of which I don't remember, then urged us to get ready to travel.

We hiked all day down hill.

Four of the Indian men and two young women came on our journey with us carrying our packs and cooking for us. Omac kept urging us on. The Indians had no problems, but I did. I thought I was in condition but I was entirely exhausted when we finally made camp. It was a permanent camp base with shelter and fire sites set up. Miguel told me it was the meeting site of Omac with the Indians at each full moon. The Indians brought supplies and Omac brought a small figurine for the Catholic priest to sell.

July 17

After our morning meal today, we left the Indians and carried our own packs—sleeping bags, light change of clothes, food tins and of course packages of thin writing paper with pencils and pens. Omac carried more than Lea, Sanchez and myself combined. And he moved with ease, clearing the lightly overgrown path ahead of him.

We cut off sharply on an angle from our campsite for much of the morning. Omac led the way with Sanchez, Lea and then myself. I counted the steps I took and wrote them down. I also noted exact directions with the everything-watch my family had given me. I also noted our altitude. Most of the afternoon we traveled upward. Near evening we moved in a zigzag path. Lea and I were lagging behind so Omac took on more of our gear. I've never seen anyone so strong—and Omac is supposed to be old.

We had been moving along a ledge, black sheer rock hovering over us, when Omac stopped. On a ledge above him he moved two large rocks apart about ten feet. He pushed on the rock wall. A huge portion of the wall nearly twenty feet high pivoted like a revolving door about four feet above him. He easily climbed up and helped each of us up and through the opening into a huge grotto.

As we entered we were startled to see our reflections in a pure black polished wall in front of us.

"To stop the Devil,"Omac said in Spanish. "He can't remain himself when he sees himself."

It sent shivers down me. I had not expected Omac to speak of the Devil. I wondered what we had gotten ourselves into. It put a whole different focus on the exploration.

As we followed Omac into the cave, I became aware of an unusual and dim light coming from somewhere above. When we became used to the light, we could see the cave was about a hundred feet long and about forty feet high. But along the walls reaching up about twenty feet were indentation and notches that were filled with artifacts like those the priest had shown us at the village. These were mostly gold and the inlaid green stones I now knew were emeralds. There were all types of small statues, figurines, pots, vases, symbols, plates, bowls, jugs and other types of artwork. There seemed to be thousands of them. Most looked as if they were gold and emerald. When we examined them, we found that they were.

I think we all knew immediately that this was the treasure that Sanchez had said we would find.

It was getting dark and Omac made a fire from wood that was stored at the end of the room. We ate from some of the stores Omac had stashed in the cave in a pyramidal shaped storage bin. The food was delicious.

We laid out our sleeping bags. Omac went to sleep on a mat in the corner. We were given a pot for our toilet, which we used in a dark corner.

It's been a wonderfully exciting day!

July 18

We awoke this morning when the outside sun light came streaming through the openings at the top of the cave.

We began wandering around looking at the artifacts.

It was Sanchez who first noticed the smell of smoke.

It was Omac. He was literally burning up.

He was sitting in the middle of the cave with blue-white flames coming from him in every direction through his poncho.

Sanchez tore off his own poncho and rushed to him. But the huge Omac waved him back. Omac mumbled a few words to him in Spanish about a passageway and I thought he pointed toward me.

Then Omac looked skyward and raised both arms upward saying in Spanish, "It is finished."

Immediately Omac's entire body, poncho and head burst into flame. In an unbelievably short time he disintegrated. In less than a few tortuous minutes all that was left of Omac was a pile of ashes, some scorched shreds of his poncho and his gold and emerald hair band, only slightly out of shape, resting on his remains. His ashes were almost six inches deep and nearly a yard wide. The smell was ghastly.

I had heard of people burning up by interior spontaneous combustion. I had heard of it happening in every part of the world, but I never thought I would see it. It was gruesome.

Omac's burning left us all in shock.

We sat at a distance looking at Omac's remains. The odor coming from them continued to be putrid.

Lea slid over to me and I held her until she slept.

The light that came from the upper sides of the cave faded and then brightened just a bit. I figured the moon was coming out through the openings in the upper part of the cave room. At least I'm finding it enough by which to write.

July 19

This morning Lea and I woke up together. Sanchez had been up before us and had laid our back packs near us. He was visually searching Omac's ashes and had set several objects from the walls around his remains. One was a large bowl. I realized he was preparing to put what was left of Omac into it. But he did not.

Lea said we should have a prayer, and she said it.

We were all listless all day. We kept staring at Omac's remains and wondering what to do next.

We wandered around the cave looking at the artifacts sitting in the indentations of the walls. There were golden plates, urns, mugs, bowls, creature and human forms, etc., almost all emerald encrusted. There was all sorts of pottery decorated in gold and emeralds. It is a fabulous find. I keep wondering why Omac brought us here.

Omac kept wandering through my mind all day as we searched the cave. Where did he come from? Why was he so gigantic? What was a white man doing here surrounded by Indians? How old was he? The Catholic priest had said he was ancient. The Indian who was an aide to the priest had told us he was around before their great grandfathers and he had come from the North. They said he had not changed in looks for as long as they knew him. He had always had a white beard.

Why did he seem to trust us? The stuff in this cave is worth a fortune. Why us? Why did he talk of the Devil? That scared me.

Why did he burn up? Why did he say, "It is finished." Those were the words Christ used when he died on the cross.

I'm feeling more and more shaky about this whole adventure. I have a feeling something very unusual is going to happen. It's eerie. I am sure Lea and Miguel are feeling some of the same things.

Maybe tomorrow—or tonight we'll find out.

July 20

I awoke this morning after having all sorts of weird dreams. I was almost afraid to open my eyes.

But it didn't turn out that way.

I can truthfully say that today was the day that of all the amazing and marvelous adventures I have ever had, including yesterday, this was the ultimate.

After gulping our unappetizing breakfast, we again began searching along the walls of the cave of fabulous golden artifacts, feeling each crevice to find an opening. In an enlarged indentation of one of the cave walls suddenly my hand and arm seemed to vanish. I put my flashlight around the bend and pressed my hand against where the rock wall was showing, but no light penetrated. I shoved the flashlight at the wall, and it and my hand disappeared with no light showing. It was as if I had submerged my hand into an inky liquid. But there was no wetness, only extreme cold. It was as if my forearm had passed through a solid wall. It was eerie.

I pulled back with a jerk. The stone structure had not moved. I felt my head and body drain of blood. I've been in danger of my life several times but never have I felt such fear. I had read of entering the third dimension and here it was.

Gathering my composure, I softly called to Miguel and Lea who came to me at once.

Together we studied the side of the inversion in the wall that had seemingly absorbed my arm. Never had I lacked for an adventurous nature, until then. I felt fear of an unusual kind. There appeared to be no immediate danger to my person. No animal or person was attacking me, as had happened many times. I was not falling through space from the side of a mountain or in a disabled plane, as had occurred twice. Or was there a hint of the other perils that dotted my lifestyle. Always I had been in control of my faculties that eventually rescued me.

But now it was different.

I remember shaking uncontrollably. It was the terror of the unknown!

I told Sanchez to touch the wall.

I watched as he felt the strange partition. His forearm vanished into it, just as had occurred to me. But his motion carried him forward and his entire body seemed to melt into what looked like solid rock. I yelled and jumped back into Lea, as I thought Sanchez had been pulled.

I have to admit Lea seemed to be less afraid than I was as she moved toward the wall just as Sanchez came back standing half outside and half dissolved. He shouted to us about a passage that was beyond and melted back into what looked like a granite wall.

This time Lea and I followed him.

The illusion of a rock wall was perfect. For several feet the passageway was black. No light came in and it was so cold it reminded me of a meat freezer. Suddenly, however, we came into light and two figures flashed before me. This time I lost control of my bladder. But then I realized it was a reflection of myself and Lea on a wall surface that was like a mirror. I remembered Omac saying that the Devil couldn't see himself and remain himself.

The thrill I had felt when we first entered the outer cave of gold figurines was in no way comparable to the sensation I felt as we came into the gigantic pyramidal chamber.

It was dazzling! Brilliant light filled the immense room. The four-sided pyramid, as large as three football fields laid side by side, including both the end zones with the four triangular walls pointing up nearly two hundred feet to its vortex, was covered with gold including the floor.

But even more spectacular were the geometric formations sitting like a military graveyard centered in the middle of the floor. But instead of tombstones there were row upon row of golden blocks standing somewhat taller than myself and approximately four feet square. It flashed through my mind that if the blocks were solid gold there was perhaps as much gold here as had ever been discovered in all time in all of the rest of the earth.

I believed at once it was the true El Dorado!

We stood aghast for a long instant and then started shouting and hugging each other and dancing about.

I knew, even if the gold only covered hidden rocks, it was a giant find. I quick counted over thirty pillars facing us and if squared meant nearly a thousand blocks.

Then Sanchez and I went like children from one immense square column of gold to the next, caressing each as a sheik might do to his harem of nude wives. We did this over and over again, as well as rubbing the walls and floor of the wondrous room.

It was the practical Lea who found the water. Along the wall, by my watch, was east, a small gusher of water sprang from an indentation in the floor and a stream flowed for several yards along a foot deep and two foot-wide golden gutter. Then it disappeared into a crevice just large enough for the water to pass through.

Lea had tasted it and found it cold and pure.

I quickly figured we could use it as a toilet too where it dropped into the crevice.

Lea said she would wash my clothes as I was beginning to stink.

The light slowly became even more brilliant. It came into concealed openings near the top of the ceiling. But the reflection on the gold made the room literally radiant. It was not subdued as in the outer cave that was of smooth rock.

We began to search the room and finally counted thirty-two rows of thirty two rows of columns of gold for a total of one thousand twenty four. We also found four more lying on their side stacked against the far wall from the entrance. And Lea found two others near the entrance but in a corner that stood upright. There was a large bin with dried food.

The pyramid began to give less of a glow and we realized the sun must have passed over to the far side of the mountain.

Before nightfall and before we forgot where the opening was, Sanchez passed through its inky blackness to bring the rest of our gear and food into the pyramid from the cave of artifacts. I stood by the passageway in the cave while Sanchez and Lea paid their respects to the ashes of Omac and brought in the packs.

We settled our equipment by the stream.

It was then Lea spotted two fish swimming in the water down the stream. She yelled to us and we each grabbed at them and finally caught one as the other escaped down the exit crevice.

The fish was not large but we cleaned it and ate it raw along with some of our other canned goods. It was a feast.

We sat and chatted like magpies about our discovery as we ate. Our conversation centered around how we would ever get our fortune out of the pyramid and cave. We talked until it grew fairly dark and our thoughts turned to other things such as finally taking a bath.

We let Miguel take his bath first and wash his clothes while we staked out an area behind the fourth row of gold columns. He settled in down the stream from us behind the eighth columns.

Lea and I bathed and washed our clothes together in the dim light. We cavorted like a couple of newlyweds. In the shadowy light she was very appealing and the day ended gloriously.

Lea fell asleep in her own pack as the moon from outside began to lighten the pyramid.

I sat and wrote of the day. It is a good thing that Lea brought plenty of paper as I had to again steal some from her to write all the marvelous things that have happened.

July 27

This morning I slowly awoke with a feeling of alarm.

I quickly assessed where I was. I did not stir for from past experience I felt I might be in danger. I looked through a slit of one eye and found myself observing Miguel Sanchez who was already up, bending over his knapsack and standing down by the stream's end. Occasionally and mysteriously he kept looking over his shoulder at me.

Suddenly he seemed to find what he wanted. When he stood, I saw he had his hatchet in one hand and his long knife in the other. He started to come toward our columns with what appeared to be an almost demonic look on his face and in his eyes.

I quickly deduced that Sanchez had gold fever. The cache we found, he figured, was going to be all his.

I had to get out of the sleeping bag. I didn't know if I had a chance as I was bound by the sides of the bed sack. I always carried a sheathed knife to sleep with me, as I had had too many snakes or other varmints as bedfellows.

I grasped the knife and slipped it loose. I slid the zippered side of the bag open. I lept upright from my bed roll and yelled to Lea.

I startled Sanchez, but a smile came on his scraggly face as he saw my knife.

"You thought of the same thing I did, right?" he said. "Let's see if these things are solid gold or not."

Then he turned and began chipping away at the corner gold column with his long knife and hitting it with his hatchet to send it deep into the block.

I watched, fascinated by this turn of events.

I didn't tell Miguel how close I came to stabbing him this morning.

But far as I could tell, from his chipping and cutting, the columns were solid gold.

We knew enough gold was not our problem. How to move it was.

Then that type of worry changed.

We had not been curious about the upper part of the blocks as they were taller by far than our eye level. None of us had even thought of looking at their surfaces.

Miguel was first to make the discovery. Without much thought of what he was doing, he used the indentation in the block he had carved out and he sprung up to the upper surface of the column and began looking around. He let out a sudden cry.

He yelled to us that there was some sort of inscriptions on the top of the golden blocks.

I slammed my knife deep within the next adjoining column, and using it as a step I clawed to the top of that surface and sat across from Sanchez. I pulled Lea up. We had to hold on, for now we realized the upper surfaces were slightly slanted and the gold was slick.

We all realized almost at once that the writing on top of the golden blocks were the same hieroglyphics that were from the two pages of the faded papers that Miguel had showed Lea and me to finance and make this journey. Those were the same two pages that probably had been translated into Spanish.

This is what Omac had brought us here for. It wasn't the gold.

We spent the rest of the day climbing from pillar to pillar and shouting to each other.

It is a fact that there could be few others more qualified to decipher the hieroglyphics than the three of us. We are all students of ancient Egyptian, Greek, Hebrew, and other Semitic languages. We all know Spanish and English. Lea knows many many South Sea Island writings. I know the European and many African languages. Sanchez knows a smattering of many South American Indian phrases and symbols. He is also supposedly an expert on the Mayan writings. Omac chose a splendid group to translate the writings.

July 28

Today Sanchez confessed he could read much of the hieroglyphics.

The writings were similar to his tribe's ancient language that the Catholic priest had in his library. He had known what the first two pages were, but he did not know they were the same as the hieroglyphics.

We spent the day translating, which we decided to first do in English.

Sanchez had not let Lea or me fully look at the the the sheets of manuscript he had. But I was not too surprised at the translation about The Metatron. It was Lea who translated the name Metatron into English from Spanish because she remembered that name for the first Angel of God from somewhere in her study of religions.

July 29

I was not expecting the translation today about God, El, the force and the Holy Spirit. I don't know what I was expecting from The Metatron's hieroglyphics but it certainly wasn't the Holy Spirit—God maybe. I guess I really expected something about aliens from another world or something like an ancient race perhaps from Atlantis. I have never been very prone to religion. I've seen so many different ones in my travels that, unlike Lea, I've become very skeptical. I also am not an atheist either. I have always believed in a God—especially when I'm in trouble—which has been quite often in my travels. And when Omac spoke of the Devil I was certainly willing to listen. But again now that

I've seen Omac—and the way he died—and here we are in this golden pyramid and the hieroglyphics are on these columns of gold, I have to at least keep an open mind.

Lea and Sanchez were very excited.

July 30

Lea and Sanchez are doing most of the translating. I'm going back over their work and learning the symbols. With Sanchez's knowledge of the basic hieroglyphs it is quite amazing how quickly we are catching on to what would otherwise be almost impossible to interpret. The Metatron's graphics are so easy to picture that the translation is quite easy. Even I have caught a great many words and meanings that Lea and Sanchez missed. We all agreed that the Eye of God, the Mind of God and things were correct. We agreed that Lea and Sanchez would translate and I would edit by going back over the hieroglyphics.

August 1

We realized today we had to be frugal with paper and pencils. We agreed to print the translations as small as possible. We have less than 100 sheets and 10 boxes of pencils. I agreed to do less writing in this diary and condense pages and even using pages with space on former days.

August 2

Tonight the light in the pyramid is very bright. Sanchez remembered Omac always met the transporters from the village at their rendezvous at the full moon and exchanged golden items for supplies. I fooled with my everything watch and figured August 3, 1955 was tomorrow night. I dug out the directions I had jotted down on a piece of Lea's paper when we came with Omac. We have decided to take nothing with us but water, a small amount of food and all our empty knapsacks—and our translations, just in case. We'll pick up some gold object on our way out tomorrow through the outer cave.

August 3 and 4

Met yesterday at the meeting place with the villagers just as the sun set and the full moon appeared. I remembered the full moon always rises as the sun sets. Now I wondered if this was one of God's works or just something that happened in time. A few days ago I wouldn't have given it a second thought.

We were elated to see the Indians and greeted them with shouts of joy. We were really happy to be there. My directions proved to be very good. I had not only counted steps and noted directions with my everything watch, when we followed Omac to the cave, I had also secured pieces of paper that I had run through with a stick that pointed any change in directions.

On this trip I had led the first hour and when I found the first piece of paper pierced by a stick I let out such a screech that Lea and Sanchez thought I'd been hurt. My directions were great.

But the trip was exhausting. We decided to spend the day resting and start back early in the morning. We had each taken turns cutting the underbrush but being sixty doesn't help. Of course the feast the Indians had for us last night with the intoxicating drinks doesn't help.

We had agreed not to tell anyone that Omac was dead for fear they might follow us or may not bring supplies next time. We did ask if the priest could find us more paper and writing tools.

Better quit writing today as Lea is giving me a stare.

August 5 and 6

We got back OK. Exhausted again.

August 7

Today we got in an argument about the translations—mostly Lea and Sanchez. Their voices reverberated in the huge pyramidal cavern. Both went to sleep mad. I tried to intervene but only stopped the shouting.

August 8

There is still a lot of tension between Lea and Sanchez. I am very amazed at the translations—especially the Trinity. Of course, it is much different than Lea or Sanchez had believed. I was only slightly aware of what they had believed.

August 9

I am really beginning to get the hang of the hieroglyphics. I always was quick at understanding different languages. I translated the I AM and Lea THE WORD. Lea thinks that AMILOUS is the correct translation of the third part of the TRINITY. She remembered reading something similar someplace and it seems right.

August 10

I'm translating the hieroglyphics myself with the help of Sanchez and Lea. Lea and Sanchez are still at odds but we all agree on the word RENEWAL. We completed 15 of the column top hieroglyphics today. Fantastic!

August 11

Lea picked up my diary tonight and was furious that I wasted so much paper and pencils writing instead of saving for the Revelations.

August 12 to September 4

It seems like a lot has happened since August 11. The priest found another 90 pages of paper, some his own personal stationery. We had taken a half dozen golden art objects to the villagers. I didn't drink so much this time, although I certainly felt like it after deciphering the last batch of hieroglyphics. We are really moving along. We are decoding up to 20 columns a day. Showing THE WORD, Angels, Souls, Archangels, the beginning of life on earth. Agreeing to call passive life planal and aggressive life animal. The Holy Spirit and water. The Amilous and blood. Michael, Bael and Belzebel. Bael and the creation of dinosaurs? And their destruction. Really interesting. What's next?

We also decided to place the ashes of Omac in a beautiful golden, emerald-encrusted bowl. From the time of his spontaneous combustion Omac's ashes had settled to almost an inch of residue which probably was mostly clothing. But we scooped up what we could and set the jar on an empty shelf. We didn't know what we should do, but we all said a silent prayer. We all—with reservations—felt that Omac was probably The Metatron using one of his many names.

September 5

We had a meeting and agreed to work long and hard with an occasional day off. Sanchez will take a different day than Lea and myself.

September 6 to 7

I was surprised about the Heaven of the Lord God. Lea chided me and said she and a lot of preachers had been right all the time.

September 8

Lea translated and insisted the name that was given Bael was the D-Evil. We humored her. Maybe she's right and that's where it came from.

September 9

Wish we didn't have so much raw fish. They keep coming down the stream. We're all tired of the smoked meats the villagers bring. It's lucky everything keeps well in the pyramid. Even the fruits and also the vegetables. But the variety of food certainly isn't gourmet. It was our day off and we enjoyed it.

September 10 to 11

Souls. Interesting. Lea and I are amazed at how well we are able to decipher the hieroglyphics. We agree that there is more to our ability than we feel is normal. Sanchez of course is able to use the language that was used in his village and helps us out on an amazing amount of words. But both Lea and I seem to have meanings flash into our minds and we have no idea why. Lea, of course, was a student of religions but the way the names of Angels and Archangels appear in her conscious amazes her. We are all aware—even Sanchez—that sometimes we are almost in a trance as we translate. When we finish, I'll think about it more.

September 12

Now we know who the first human-like creatures were. We let Lea call them Amen. No more comment!

September 13 to 14

The Amens were certainly astonishing to all of us.

September 15 to 17

Bael was certainly a Devil.

September 18 to 19

These were astonishing days. Nobody has taken a day off for ten days. This seems to be where Genesis in the Torah or Old Testament started. Lea and Sanchez—and I guess me—were ecstatic and amazed. These translations are astonishing. Lea says these prove the Creation as shown in the Bible but there was just a great period of time before the first verse in the Bible.

This is where the billions of years advocated by scientists meet with Creation in the Bible. They are both right! What a discovery! What a find! There seems to be 144,000 Adams and Eves, however.

September 20

Here is the expulsion of Baal to the Void. It also seems important that Souls begin entering Man.

September 21

Now we know Angels were on Earth directing men and women. We now know why there may be separate races of Man.

September 22

We all decided to take the day off. It was a fabulous day of washing clothes, bathing and relaxing and talking.

Sanchez mentioned he had flashes of insight into words and whole phrases just like Lea and I had.

Looking forward to a great night.

September 23 to 26

These have been exciting days. Lea and Sanchez have been ecstatic and I guess I have, too.

Now we know where the pervasive myths about the gigantic turmoil, conflict, battle and final separation between God and the Devil, Satan-Bael come from. Now we know how Bael the great Archangel duped nearly a third of the Angels and almost all of the Souls to cross over to him. And how Michael, The Metatron and Amilous saved many. And how the "Fallen Angels" were cast upon the Earth in Atla— Atlantis.

September 27

And how Amilous and then the Amen tried to help the Souls.

September 28

Man shall be a Living Soul of flesh and blood and his Breath shall Know the Spirit of Amen from God to Guide him.

Lea says this is profound. This is what great religions and also psychiatrists extol—flesh, soul and higher spirit or flesh, ego and super ego. Makes some sense.

September 29
Realignment of the Earth—again.

September 30
We decided to rest. Tomorrow we go to pick up supplies. We discussed what we have translated so far. This is really going to upset a lot of thinking about everything before what everyone thought was the first civilization. But it also confirms a lot of beliefs.

October 1 to 2
We took many golden pieces to the Indians for the priest and also asked the transporters to have him save some for us. The Indians were asking a lot of questions about Omac. Sanchez did a good job of fending off their questions.

October 3
We decided that we couldn't put off the inquiry by the Indians of why Omac did not come with us much longer. We all agreed to speed up as much as possible the deciphering of the writings.

We were tired from the trip but the golden pyramid seems to have redemptive powers. We began work this afternoon. Maybe we can finish by the next full moon—blue moon October 30.

October 4 to 14
It's been like translating from the second chapter of Genesis with the formation of the real Adam and then Eve. Then another deceit by Baal of the Lord God through Eve. And on through to Noah. With a few surprises like the Angels taking women for wives and bearing Nephilim and Raphiem, the giants as told in the Bible. The Metatron coming to Earth as Enoch. The partial sinking of Atlantis. The other Noah—Xisuturous—and Og. Og duping Noah with toxic drink.

We took the day off so I'm catching up.

October 15 to 16

The Lord God abandons Earth because Mankind regenerates nearly as before. Belzues and Og help in control and reproduction. Belzues names himself Zeus.

October 17

Amilous comes to Earth as the Angel Ra but is put to death by the Fallen Angels.

October 18 to 23

We finished the translations this afternoon. We immediately began preparations to leave.

   These past few days have been eye-opening with the Angels leaving Earth and the further destruction of Earth by Baal—especially Atlantis and other great sections of land. The reawakening of Noah and his sons. The Tower of Babel. The coming of The Metatron and Sandalphon to Earth.

October 24

We decided to wait until tomorrow to leave. That is when we found the directions to another cave. We decided against going into it at this time but to return later. The directions are on the side of the last column.

October 25

We arrived at the meeting place in early evening. We carried as many golden objects as could. We will leave most of them here for the villagers to come and carry back. We will take what we have on the plane plus some from the priest. We're really going to be short on food tomorrow so we hope we make the village.

   What a fascinating adventure this has been. We are all elated and wondering what the world will think of our discovery. Lea says she may change some of the Angels' names when she rereads her books but the rest should stay much the same as translated.

   We paid our last respects to Omac—The Metatron?—when we left. We decided we will tell the priest of the way he died.

October 28

It's terrible! Son Scott is dead. Killed by lightning they said. Daughter Lyn has been trying to find us for three weeks. Priest just happened to be listening to news on the radio and heard the appeal to find us. Terrible, terrible, terrible.

And it took a day to get the plane ready to go. But we're on our way.

(This was the end of the diary that was given to me. Copies of the original diary must have been burned at the publishing firm when it was being shown to Mrs. Wallace. And as Per Sornson reported, the plane was struck by lightning and crashed but all escaped alive. The death of Lea with electricity during a bath was a further mystery.)

Revelations of
The Metatron

Revelations of The Metatron

I am The Metatron—first Angel and Scribe of God, El, Creator and
   Almighty Spirit.
I was Conceived in body on this part of Earth to Lead, Teach and Train
Building to those who Survived the Great Floods.
My twin the Sandalphon, the Dark One, was also Formed in body. But
   she is Traveling to another part of Earth to do as I.[4]
Before I do my mission, as the Scribe of God, El, of the I AM, I will
Leave Knowledge of the TIME of I AM.
I am The Metatron, Scribe of God, El.

The Holy Being
The Great Spirit, Almighty God, El
Creator and Maker of the many Heavens,
Who through the force, was ever Expanding with Knowledge and Emotions,
Felt Loneliness.

God, El,
By the Mind of God and the Eye of God, with the force,
Created the Holy One from a part of Himself,
To Love and in Return Love and Adore Him.

Though the Almighty Spirit was Complete with all Emotions—
For all Emotions were Given to God, El, from before—
He Gave to the Holy Spirit, through the force, all the positive emotions
But Not those that were Related to Desire for Power.

All the negative Emotions
Were Endowed to the Holy One
That were Attached with Love—
Such as Reception, Honor and Adoration.

But Negative Emotions, such as
Vanity, Greed, Lust, Hatred, Jealousy, Despair—all later Known as Evil—
Were Not Given to the Holy Spirit.
And the Evil was Cast into the Void.

For every positive in all the World, there must be a like amount of negative
To Keep the force in balance.
Love is both positive and negative and is the link of all Emotions.
And the Holy One was Filled with Love.

Then the Maker of All Gave great Knowledge and Energy from Himself,
With the force, through the Mind of God and the Eye of God,[5]
To the Holy One to Understand all things that had been Created.
And the Holy Spirit Became a Being.

God, El,
Felt great Satisfaction with the Holy Being.
And it was as if they were one—
Though they were Not.

Then the Creator of All, Who,
Through the Mind of God and the Eye of God, Controls the Rhythm of
    the force,
Continued to Expand the Galaxies of the Universe into the Heavens,
For Himself and the Pleasures of the Holy One. And it was Good.

Things[6]
Now each and every thing in the Heavens, no matter how small,
Knows its vibration with the Energy of God
Which is Set in Attunement through the Mind of God and the Eye of God,
With the Power of the force.

The Almighty is Aware of the most minute of things.
When the Almighty Spirit,
Through the Mind and the Eye of God, with the force,
Commands any thing to Go or Do, it Does.

Each thing knows its place
At a specific Time
In God's Creation—
And God Knows its Situation with all other things.

In the Void,
Even before a thing is Formed by the ever expanding Light,
And prior to its set vibration in the harmony of that which Is,
There is an Anticipation of its Awareness by the Maker.

In all the Void,
There is a Yearning
To be part of the Universes of the Heavens,
And to Become a thing.

Though many things were from Before,
The Mind of God and the Eye of God are ever Abstracting new things,
With the force,
Controlled by the Great Spirit.

Each thing has its own individuality—even if ever so slight a variation—
Down to the most diminutive of entities.
Even then the Conceptuality of God in this World Cannot be Compre-
    hended—
For it is Beyond.

The Holy One's Conception
The Holy Being Enjoyed and Admired each object
That was made by the Almighty, with the force.
But the Holy One was Not Able to Form any thing or be part of
The Creator's Originality and Felt the lack of Fulfillment.

God, El, was Aware of these Emotions of the Holy Spirit,
And Conveyed that He would Bring into being, through the force,
Any Imaginable thing that the Mind of the Holy One could Conceive,
Which was of a clear and precise Perception.

The Holy Spirit was Filled with Elation
By the Idea of doing that which had never been done before
And Gave profound Thought
To the favor of the Almighty.

As was the nature of the Holy Being,
The Creation
Would have to be something
That would be wholly Pleasing to God.

It must be a thing
That would Show the Love, Honor and Adoration
For the Almighty
By the Holy Spirit.

That which would Come Forth
Must be something
That would Bring great Pleasure and Happiness to the Maker of All.
It must be something that had never been Formed before.

Therefore,
The Holy Spirit
Took much time
In Arriving at a Decision.

This Pleased the Omniscient One,
For He had Feared the Vision of the Holy One
Might be such that He might have to Bring Forth
Something that was an Abomination.

God's Love
For the Holy Spirit
Was such
That He did Not Want this to happen.

The Holy One
Reflected upon the Almighty
And the Joy that Flowed
Between them.

In their Form
Of Spirit Essence
They would Move and Mingle through and with each other
As the mists of the Universes.

Even though the Omnipresent One was the vastness of all,
They were as one,
Never ceasing, wafting through the Heavens
Exchanging their Emotions.

Though the Being of God Encompassed all the Emotions,
And the Emotions of the Holy Spirit were limited to those of the most
    Pure
They seemed to have No separation—
And yet they were Each Entities.

Upon this the Holy One Contemplated.
In all of the Creation of the Universes and the Heavens,
Never
Had the Almighty Made any other like the Holy Spirit.

The most magnificent Grace
In all of the Eternity of God, El,
Was the Manifestation itself,
Of the Holy Being.
The Omnipotent One, El,
Had taken a part of Himself
To Make a companion to Love
And in return be Loved.

The Vision of Sacrifice to Form the Third Being
Then the Holy One
Envisioned
That which could be Offered
To Show the ultimate Love of God.

It would be the Sacrificing of half of the Self
To Form another Spirit Being,
So that the Almighty God would have two Beings
Who would Love, Honor and Adore Him and Enjoy the Wonders of his
     Creation

God, El,
Knowing All,
Was Overjoyed
With such an Inspiration.

When the Creator
Revealed an even deeper Desire.
He would Share in the Sacrificial-Creation
With the Holy Spirit.

God, El
Would Give a part of Himself
Equal to that
Which would be Surrendered by the Holy One.

From the Wisdom
Of God, El,
Came
The great Thought.

A portion of His Great Spirit,
Not Separated and in His true nature,
Equal to that of the Holy Spirit
Would be Utilized to Form the Being that would be the Third.

That Part of the Almighty
That would help Create the Third
Would be Known as
The Lord of God or Lord God.

The Lord of God, The Holy One and The New Spirit
Would Form a Trinity of Equals in Spirit.
The New Spirit Being
Would be the Third of the Trinity.[7]

He would be Formed
From one third of the Lord of God
And one third
Of the Holy Spirit.

Thus,
One Half of the New Third's total Being
Would be as, and from, that part of God, The Lord of God.
And one half of the Third's Being, as and from, the Holy Spirit.

Thus Equal to the Spirit of the Lord God
And to the Holy Spirit
Would be the Essence of the Third.
But Each would be of a different nature.

Note: This etching was on the golden stand. The three center wavy
lines were equal. The long one, of which the center one was a
part of, appeared to be infinite.[8]—Translator

Amilous—Son of God

Then the Creator,
With the Mind and Eye of God
And with that of the Holy Spirit,
Through the force,

Brought Forth from the Essence Spirit of Himself, The Lord of God,
And from the Essence of the Spirit of the Holy One,
The New Spirit Being
That was Third.

The new Being
Was the sum total of
Emotions, Knowledge, Energy and Spirit Essence
As Endowed by the Holy One and the Lord of God.

From the Lord God
The Third was Filled with vast Knowledge, Energy and Emotions
That were of the enormous range of God,
But much less in magnitude.

The extreme Emotions of the Third,
Given by the Lord God,
Were modified
By the nature of the Holy Spirit.

Thus such Emotions as Desire for Power
And those of Evil—
Greed, Anger, Lust, Hatred, Jealousy, Vanity and Despair
Were Subdued.

Then the Almighty, in His Joy, made it Known to the Holy One
And to All that had been Created and all that was in the Void,
That the Third Being
Would be known as the Son of God.

His name
Was to be Amilous,[9]
Which means
Son of I AM.

I AM and THE WORD
For the first time,
God, El,
Partially Revealed the Knowledge of
The I AM.

Because of That which WAS Before, I AM,
I AM was THE WORD Before
It was and Is
The Beginning of this TIME.

But the I AM was Not the Infinite Beginning
Or will it Be the Infinite End,
For the I AM will Renew once again
At the End of this TIME.

When the positive
Becomes the negative,
The Thrust
Will Become the Reception.

The Father of All in the I AM
Will Transmute into the Cosmic Egg of the RENEWAL.
And the Father
Will Become the Mother of ALL.

Then the I AM
Will no longer Be,
But will be
THE WORD.

I, El, God of the I AM[10]
Will be Known by ninety nine Names in this TIME,
and the Hundredth will be THE WORD[11]
That will Renew into that which will Be.

When IT is Sounded,
All that are Called,
Will Unify with THE WORD
At RENEWAL.

"Henceforth, the Son of God, The Amilous, The Son of I AM,
Is Entrusted with THE NEW WORD.
 THE WORD is with the Son of God
Until the End of I AM.

And when the Son of I AM Speaks the Hundredth Name,
Which is THE WORD,
All that will be renewed from the I AM will Merge into THE WORD—
And no thing or being shall Prevail against THE WORD."

"That which is in the Void
Shall not Renew
But may Hope for its Reward
In the RENEWAL."

"Thus the Amilous,
The Son of God, the Son of I AM
And THE WORD,
Are all the Same."

Now even then,
When they became Aware of this great Knowledge
There were mysteries that the Amilous and the Holy One
Did not yet Understand.

Then the Creator Returned to the Forming of the Heavens.
And the Amilous and the Holy Spirit
Were Amazed at the Splendor of the things that Flowed
From the Mind of God and the Eye of God.

During the eons of Time
The Amilous
And Holy Spirit
Grew in Knowledge and Emotions.

But Time was Not important,
Except when it Related to Energy, Matter and things
With the Light against
The Darkness of the Abyss.

Angels
Now the Almighty
Was Pleased with the Companionship of the Holy Spirit and the
    Amilous.
He Enjoyed the Love and Adoration
That Flowed between them.

Such was His Satisfaction
That the Omnipotent One
Began Thinking of other Beings that might be Pleasing
Not Only to Himself but also to the Son and the Holy One.

While in Full Contemplation
He Brought Forth
Through the Mind of God with the force,
Two Spirit Beings.

They Came fully from Himself.
They were Not as major in degree as were the Trinity.
But they were Given
Full range of Emotions, Energy and great Knowledge.

He
Named them Angels,
Meaning
Lesser sons of El.

One He called The Metatron,[12]
Meaning first,
and the other the Sandalphon,[13]
Meaning second.

And their main difference,
Though their nature of unique,
Was that the Sandalphon was Endowed with less of the Emotions
Related to Thrust and Power.

Thus The Metatron was Given
The full and vast range of Emotion
As God, El,
And the Lord of God.

But The Metatron
Was an unmeasurable less Spirit
Than the Almighty—
Or any of the Trinity.

Then with intense Concentration
Through the Mind and Eye of God with the force,
The Creator Brought Forth, from Himself,
A multitude of Angel Spirits.

They filled
The many Heavens
With their Love, Adoration, Brilliance
And Companionship.

Now this was in the Time of the Seventh Heaven
And Angels were as many
As the many great Forms in the Seventh Heaven.
And they were Divided into the eleven Orders of Angels.[14]

Five Orders
Were in the Seventh Heaven—
The Mighty Seraphim, Headed by Sammael;
The Splendid Cherubim, Headed by Ophaniel;

The Thrones, Headed by Zaphkiel;
The Crowns, Headed by Anaphiel;
The Potentates, with Chief Ariel,
And they Ruled the Thrones and Crowns.

In the Sixth Heaven
Were the forceful Dominations, with Chief Zadkiel;
The Fifth Heaven,
The Principalities, with Chief Aniel;

The Fourth Heaven,
The Powers, with Chief Camael;
The Third Heaven,
The Choirs, with Chief Radueriel;

The Second Heaven,
The Scribes, with Chief Vretael;
And the First Heaven
The Virtues, with Chief Sabrael.

Some Angels were Charged with Energy,
Some Filled with great Knowledge, some with vast Emotions
Some with all of these and some with little.
But each and every Angel was Unique in some way.

Only a few were Given the Desire for Power and none were Given
Those of Vanity, Greed, Anger, Lust, Hatred, Jealousy or Despair—
But The Metatron and Sandalphon.
Again all the Emotions Not Endowed were Loosed into the Void.

The Creator Called the Angels the lesser sons of God,
But El made it Known
That the Amilous was the only true Son of God of the I AM,
For He had Come from the Love of the Holy Spirit.

The Almighty
Had Symmetry in his Seven Heavens.
Thus he Desired the same for all his Beings.
Seven Orders of Angels were Placed in the Seven Heavens.

Those Angels that had been Created first, after The Metatron and San-
    dalphon
Were Broad with Knowledge, Energy and Emotions.
They were the Seraphim and they were Placed in the Seventh Heaven
With three other Orders of Angels.

And the Seraphim
Were Placed in Charge
Of all the Angel Orders in the Seventh Heaven
And this was Headed by Sammael

For the Seventh Heaven
Was next to the Void
And here was the Concentration of the newest things
Made by the Creator

The Metatron and the Sandalphon were Placed Above them all,
Next to the Trinity,
And were Given Charge of Maintaining the Harmony of the Angels
In the Heavens, with the Trinity.

The Organization
Of the Heavens
Was Pleasing
To God.

Now the Amilous
Was Absorbing the Knowledge
Of the Arrangement of All in the Heavens
Including the Angels.

All of the Angels Loved the Amilous and He Loved them.
It was He who would Intercede
If any Angel Found themselves at odds with others
For Angels each were different in Emotions, Knowledge and Energy.

But each Angel
Was Filled with Love,
For they
Had Come Directly From God.

And through the Knowledge and Teaching of the Amilous,
The Angels Found a bond of Love through the Aid of the Amilous
Or the Comfort of the Holy One,
And this Pleased God.

Souls
The Amilous, who Knew He Came from God,
Through the Lord God and from the Sacrifice of the Holy One,
Was Aware that Sacrificial-Creation
Was the most marvelous of gifts.

His nature,
Coming from both God and the Holy Spirit,
Made the Amilous Desirous to Give of Himself
For the Adoration of the Creator.

Now God was Satisfied with all of His Spirit Beings.
Each was Complimentary to the other
And all were Full of Love and Devotion to Himself
And to one another. And the Amilous Knew this.

And the Amilous Wished to Take a part of Himself—As had the Holy
    One
For his Own Creation, to Become the Son of God—To Show His Love
And Adoration for the Almighty—The Father of all things and Beings.
And God Knew of the Desire of the Amilous.

The Holy Spirit and the Amilous
Were the Greatest of all God's Glorifications in all the Heavens—
And the Angels
Were of great Companionship.

Thus the Almighty
Favored
The Thoughts of the Amilous
To Bring Forth new Beings.

His Concern
Was the Weakening of the Son of God in the Trinity.
Any Division of Self would Lessen the Powers of the Amilous.
But Sacrificial-Creation and Love were even more important.

Then all the Angels,
Knowing the Glorification of Sacrifice,
Yearned to be a part of the new Beings.
Now the Almighty was Pleased and Approved.

With the force, the Maker,
Through the Mind of God and the Eye of God
In Attune with the Amilous and each Angel,
Brought Forth the new Beings.

From each Angel He Took a small part,[15]
Fortifying each part with a minute amount from the Amilous,
And Caused the Emergence of those new Beings,
Later Called Souls.

These Beings were tiny in Essence and Spirit
And Limited in Emotional scope—
Much Less than that of their Donating Angel—
But they were Enriched by the Addition of that from the Son of God.

And they were Called Souls
From the reverse of the last of the Amilous.
For Souls were Not the sons of God,
But were of the Amilous and the Angels.

Since each Soul was from a part of an Angel,
Each Soul was Given their Angel to guard and guide them.
And the Amilous was Given Dominion over them.
And there was Joy in the Heavens—but it was short-lived.

The Mind of God
Up to the Formation of the Souls,
All had been Directly Controlled by the Mind of God and Eye of God—
And the Almighty
Knew all that Transpired.

All movement of things, and every thought and movement of Beings,
Were Tuned in to the Intellect of the Omniscient One
Who with the Mind and Eye directed all in the many Heavens—
And was Aware of the Void.

God Controlled all Power,
With the force,
That Moved all things
And was Aware and Motivated all Beings.

All Beings could Move and Enjoy the Heavens.
And there was no Command to them by God, El,
As long as each Being was in Harmony
With the I AM.

All Communications between the Beings
Was Expressed through the Mind of God and Eye of God.
These were seldom Changed,
But God was Aware of all that Occurred.

The Problems with Souls
The Serenity of the Heavens
Was Disturbed by the Souls.
Souls did Not Come Directly from God, El,
As had all other Beings.

They were miniscule, combination offshoots
Of the Amilous and the Angels
And thus
Once removed from God, El.

The Almighty was Aware of all Souls
But their Wills were Not always Attuned to the Mind and Eye of God.[16]
There was a need for Concentration
For a full Communication between the Souls and God, El.

The tiny, free-willed and free spirited Souls,
With their wide range of Energy, Emotions and Knowledge
Roamed through the Heavens
Causing ripples of trouble.

Those with high Thrust and low Fear would speed through the Galaxies.
Some, reducing themselves to the tiniest of Essence,
Would Race like rays through the great masses
Trying to avoid collision with the inner structures.

Occasionally they would become Entrapped
And only God could Free them.
Others would Pass Off into the Void
And again would have to be Rescued.

The Amilous Loved the Souls—as did all—
But they were too Perplexing even for the Amilous to Supervise
And at the same time be able to Expand His Knowledge of the Heavens,
That the Son of I AM Needed.

Nature of Beings and Things
Now
The nature of a thing or Spirit Being
Is Formulated
At its Conception.

The Holy Spirit, the Amilous, The Metatron and Sandalphon,
All of the other Angels and all after,
Have a set Relationship with the Creator
And the Almighty does Not Change this.

But a Spirit Being
May Expand its Knowledge
From the Omnipotent Mind of God and Eye of God,
That is ever present from the past and now.

All the Knowledge of the Creator
During the Time of the I AM
Is Available for all Beings
To Decipher.

All Emotions that a Being has been Endowed With
May be Expanded or Lessened, but any additional Emotions
Must be Added only by the force, to keep it in balance,
And may be Controlled by God, El.

Love is the easiest to come by,
For that which WAS Endowed Love to the I AM, in abundance,
Through the Sacrificial-Creation.
Energy is Omnipresent from the I AM.

And all of the Visualizations and Expansions of the Beings
Enhance the I AM—
And will be Known at RENEWAL
By the Word.

Thus the nature of the Souls
Was Not to be Changed.
But still the Unity of the Heavens
Was Disrupted by their Actions.

The Archangels[17]
Now God, El, had Not been Satisfied
With the Reduction of the Amilous in Relationship to the Trinity
After the Souls had been Created
From the Self of the Amilous, the Son of God.

Now the Holy One Knew,
And again Offered part of the Self
For the Creation
Of other Beings.

Then the Maker with the Mind and Eye of God, by the force,
Took a portion from each Angel, and in Cooperation with the Holy
    Spirit,
And the part of Himself, the Lord God, Conceived the Spirits
Of the Seven Archangels. And the Trinity once again was Equal.

The Archangels
Had great Knowledge, Energy and a wide range of Emotions
That were Equal to The Metatron and Sandalphon
But Above the other Angels

The Archangel, Michael,
Was the first and most God-like,
With broad and strong Emotions
And filled with Energy and Knowledge.

Just Below in these qualities
Were Gabriel, Raphael, Uriel, Baraqiel, Belzebel
and finally—and fully Equal in totality to Michael,
But with great Desire for Power—Came Bael.

Though the Holy Spirit
Was Involved with the Archangels' Creation,
It was Noted by God, El,
That they were in No way Equal to the Amilous.

They were Called sons of God, as were the Angels,
But they were Different in Authority.
They were to Aid in Control of the Souls
And Not simply to Guide them as did their Angels.

The Hierarchy of the Heavens
Then it was Decreed
By the Almighty
What the Order of Beings
Was in the Heavens:

God, El, of the I AM, the Creator,
The Trinity of Equals,
The Metatron and Sandalphon,
The Archangels of Seven.

Then Comes the Eleven Heads
Of the Eleven Orders of Angels,
Then the Angels
And finally the Souls.

Then God, El, Chose the Seventh Heaven to Unify the Trinity,
To Mediate and Direct the other Heavens with the Aid of The Metatron,
The Sandalphon, the Archangels, the Seraphim, the Cherubim, the
    Thrones,
The Dominations and the Powers, in that Order.

And the Almighty Decreed
That a Council could be Formed
With any twelve and a Leader of any of those Named
Or the Head of an Angel Order in that Heaven.

All were Pleased but Bael—
Who did Not like to be Subject
To the Amilous, The Metatron, Sandalphon
Or any of the other Archangels.

The Records
Then the Holy One Requested of the Almighty that a Record be Made
Of all things that Occurred in the Time of the I AM
And that it be Stored in the Seventh Heaven.
And God, El, Gave his Agreement.

And a Place was to be Set
In the Seventh Heaven
To Register the Happenings of All of the I AM
And Before.

Then in the Seventh Heaven, Almighty, El, Created
Through the Mind of God and the Eye of God, with the force,
The Place of Knowledge of all that Transpired During the I AM
And Retained for the Renewal.

Its Shape was Different
Than all other Forms in the Heavens—now Known as Pyramidal—
And its size was that Not Known before
In one mass.

Its Energy was Unique and it was in Total Harmony with God, El,
Through the Mind of God and Eye of God, with the force.
It was Called by God, El, the Ashkish Record.
And All were in Awe of this Creation of God.

Then the Holy One Made it Known, by the Will of the Almighty,
That all Beings in the Heavens would be Involved
In Registering the Past and Present of the Heavens of the I AM,
Even of God, El.

Then the Holy One was Given more Knowledge of the Use of the force—
As was the Amilous—and The Metatron and Sandalphon—
Who were Charged with the final Recording
With the Holy Spirit.

And the Order of Scribes,
The Angels of the Second Heaven, whose Chief was Vretrael,
Were Given the Duty
Of Helping the Registration of the Chronicles of the I AM.

Then the Holy One Gave the Archangels the Function,
With the Use of the Souls, to Name and Number all things, groups of
    things,
All masses of things, all coordinated masses, all Galaxies,
All Universes, all Heavens, each and every Being and groups of Beings.

Also each Place that each was in the World.
And each Soul's Angel would Refine the name with God, El.
For God, El, was Aware of even the minutest of things
And their places in the Heavens and Controlled each with the force.

The Archangels
Were Divided into two groups.
Gabriel, Raphael, Uriel and Baraqiel
Were to Assist the Holy Spirit, The Metatron and Sandalphon.

Michael, Belzebel and Bael
Were to Scour the Heavens with the Souls—
And with the Aid of the Angels—
To Name names and Give numbers to All and to Identify their places.

Then the Holy Spirit
With The Metatron and the Sandalphon
Began the Chronicle of All
In the Time of the I AM.

Now the Ashkish ledger[18]
Is Not
As the writing on the golden tablets before you,
But is Different.

All is Recorded
So that by Desire
All Beings in the heavens can Know,
Though they may Not Understand.

The Revelations of the Almighty
When all things and Beings were Named, Numbered and Categorized,
With their Place in the Heavens Recorded,
There Remained
The Maker of All.

All the Souls
Were Afraid
To Approach the question of
The Tabulation of God.

But Led by Michael, Bael and Belzebel,
The Metatron Asked what additional information
The Almighty Wished
In the Archives of the I AM.

Then the Creator Revealed to All,
The Knowledge of the Origination
Of the Holy One, the Amilous, the Lord God of the Trinity
And all Beings and things.

Then was Recorded from God, El,
"In this TIME,
There was the Beginning and there will be the End
Of the I AM.

But Before I AM that I AM there WAS.
And because there WAS, I AM that I AM.
And because I AM that I AM,
That which WAS is No more.

That which is NOW,
Includes all that WAS.
For All that WAS, Sacrificed All,
For that which IS—the I AM.

The PURE LIGHT through PURE LOVE
Sacrificed All that WAS
For the Light against the Void and the I AM that I AM—
And All that are Beings and things.

From the Great Concentration of All that WAS,
Came All that IS—
And yet
There is No Separation.

From that which WAS Came the Light of the I AM[19]
And the I AM is the TIME of LIGHT.
The I AM that I AM is the LIGHT of the World
And all else is Darkness and Chaos.

And that which is in the Chaos.
Can Enter the Light of the I AM
Through the Mind of God and the Eye of God
By the Great Creator Spirit, with the force.

The force
Keeps the Harmony of the I AM
Through the Mind of God and the Eye of God,
By the Almighty.

The Mind of God is Pure Thought.
And the Eye of God is Pure Vibration that Controls the Light
And also with the Waves Brings Pleasure
To all Beings in the Heavens with the Variation of vibration.

And it Attracts that in the Void,
Through the Mind of God
By the Creator,
With the force.

The Great Spirit, Almighty Creator,
Through the Mind of God and Eye of God, with the force, is the Maker
Of all thing and Beings, with All that WAS and IS NOW and SHALL BE,
Until THE WORD Ends the TIME of the I AM.

All things and Beings
Are Separate in the I AM that I AM
And yet they are Not—
For All are One with the I AM that I AM.

Only the Void is Disjoined—
And yet
Even that may Become One with the I AM that I AM,
As the LIGHT Moves Against the Darkness.

At Its End,
The I AM that I AM will Become THE WORD,
As the Great Spirit, El, was THE WORD
At the End of that which WAS.

THE WORD is with,
And will be with,
The Son of God, Son of I AM,
The Amilous.

And All
In the I AM that I AM
Will be with
THE WORD.

The Great Spirit of God, will in the TIME of I AM,
Be Known by nine-nine Names, but the Hundredth Name—THE
    WORD—
Will be the Last of the I AM that I AM
And the Beginning of the RENEWAL of THE WORD.

And the Son of God, Son of I AM,
The Amilous,
Knows THE WORD
And will say THE WORD.

And the Amilous,
With whom I am Well Pleased,
Will Choose those Beings and things for RENEWAL
And all Else will be Cast into the Chaos of the Darkness."

And All
Were Awed
At this Pronouncement
And Thought upon it.

Now Bael was Disturbed,
For he Felt it Wrong
That the Keeper of THE WORD
Was already Chosen.

Bael Knew his Knowledge was Growing at an ever increasing rate.
Perhaps in the TIME of the I AM he would Exceed the Amilous.
And God, El, Knew of Bael's Brooding
And was Not Pleased.

Restlessness of the Souls
With the Completion of the names and numbers
Of all the things, Beings and places in the Records,
The impatient Souls
Once again Filled the Heavens with Disorder.

God, El,
For the first time,
Meted out Punishment
Especially to those Souls that Went Off into the Void.

The Metatron was Designated the Enforcer.
The Souls
Began to Fear the Powers
Of The Metatron.

Michael, Belzebel and Bael,
Who had Searched the Heavens for names and numbers with the Souls,
Were Charged
With Keeping them from Disturbing the Heavens.

But the free-willed and free-spirited Souls
Enjoyed
Confusing and Taunting
The Archangels.

The three Archangels, who were supposed to be their keepers,
Were more inclined to Encourage their mischievousness
And then Bring them to The Metatron for Punishment—
Especially Belzebel and Bael. Michael was more Wont to Protect them.

Souls and the Abyss
Souls that had been Caught in the Void
For more than short periods of time
And then Rescued,
Became Wider in their Emotions.

They became Vain, Angry, Jealous, Quarrelsome, Erratic and then
    Depressed.
Bael was quick to Notice this and because of his great Intellect,
Deduced that the Souls had been Subjected to those Emotions
That had been Released into the great Abyss.

Belzebel also Observed the Change of the Souls who had Strayed
And their tendency toward a more complex and wild type nature.
He Enjoyed Watching their Punishment
And he Tormented them or Encouraged their wanderings.

Those who came under Michael's humorous and more stable personality,
Returned to a more normal state.
All of this was Heeded by God, El,
For He was Aware of all that Transpired in the Heavens.

The Almighty Decreed the Order of the Angels, Seraphim,
Headed by Sammael,
To Patrol the edges of the Seventh Heaven
To Protect the Souls from Entering the Abyss.

He Forbade the Transgression of any Being—
Even the Archangels—
To Enter into the immense Darkness
Beyond the Heavens.

Now many Wondered about the Edicts of the Almighty—
Especially Michael, Belzebel and Bael—
For they had Felt the Sensations of the different Emotions in the Chaos
When they had Swept through on a rescue mission of the Souls.

And the three were Cognizant
Of the change of nature of those Souls
That they Saved
From the Abyss.

They Knew that God, El, did not Change the nature of Beings,
But only the Beings by themselves Changed—
Or perhaps
By that which was in the Chaos.

Now God, El, was Aware
Of the Archangels' Doubts
That the Decree
Was Definite for them.

Then God
Specifically Warned the highly active trio of Curious Archangels
To Observe his Command to stay clear of the Void—
And they were Surprised at this absolute Restriction.

Though this Caution did Not bother Michael or Belzebel
The ever Inquiring and Speculative Mind of Bael
Probed for the meaning of the Command.
And the Almighty, El, was Aware.

Knowledge Given by the Almighty
And the Omniscient One
Made Known to All,
"The Light in the Heavens is in Harmony.
The Darkness of the Abyss is in Chaos.

Nothing is Created in the Void.
Any thing or Being in the Abyss
Has Entered it from the Heavens
Where it was Made

Any thing or Being that Intrudes into the Abyss
Is Buffeted by the Chaos.
And to any Being The Metatron's Punishment is a Nothing
Compared to the Torment of the Chaos.

Now the LIGHT Moves against the Darkness
And the Chaos Becomes things and are as one with the Heavens.
But Beings are Made only in the Heavens
From the Offerings of the Self from other Beings.

Now that which WAS,
With Magnificent All Encompassing Love,
Sacrificed Totally ALL
To Bring Harmony to the Chaos.

And from the Concentration of PURE LIGHT,
The Cosmic Mass that WAS,
Became
The I AM that I AM.

And the TIME of the I AM
Is the TIME of LIGHT—
And Shall Be
Until THE WORD is Spoken.

Everything that has EVER BEEN or IS, is Known by God, El.
And the Knowledge of God, El, is ever Expanding during the time of I AM.
As it Did During that which WAS,
And will Amplify in the TIME of THE WORD.

THE WORD will Renew with all of the Knowledge of that which WAS
And IS NOW and EVER SHALL BE
In the I AM.
The God-head shall Increase for the Infinity of the Chaos.

And the Keeper of THE WORD,
The Amilous, True Son of God, Son of the I AM that I AM,
Will Choose ALL that will be with Him
In the RENEWAL.

Thus
Some things will be the same
And some will be different.
And THE WORD will Make it New

But the way to RENEWAL
Is the Love of God, El, the Holy Spirit, the Amilous
And each other
And the Sacrifice for others."

And All were Astonished and Filled with Anticipation—
But Bael—
Who again was Disturbed that he had Not been Chosen
Instead of the Amilous.

Creation Continues
The Troubles with the Souls
Had Not Deterred the Creator
From the Expansion and Formation
Of His many Heavens.

The Beings were Awe-struck
By the Spectacular Beauty
Of each different Manifestation.
But God, El, Wanted something more Unusual

The Newness
Then through the Mind of God and the Eye of God
Came such a Thought of Newness
That in all of the Eternity of the I AM,
Since the Beginning of the Creations during the TIME of I AM,

Since that which WAS,
Which Encompassed areas of Time,
That none of the Beings in Heaven
Could Understand—

Never before, Not even the Bringing Forth
Of the Holy Spirit, the Lord God and the Amilous—
For they were Divisions of Spirit
As He was of that which WAS—

Not
In All of TIME
Had there been such a Vision
So gloriously different,

All previous Creations were either of living Spirit
Or those things that performed
When sent in motion by the Creator
With the force.

The Newness was to be such
That it Never before had been Envisioned.
It would be a combination of a thing and a Being.
It would be a thing that Lived.

All Spirits Lived and had Essence,
And all things were a part of the total of the I AM.
But this would have mass and Live—but Not with Spirit—
But would still be part of the I AM and have Energy.

The Mind of God and the Eye of God
Were so intensely Concentrated on the Idea of the Creator, El,
That all the Beings
Perceived His Contemplation—

And things were also Aware,
For they were part of the I AM.
But none
Knew what to Anticipate.

With things,
The Creator had always been the most Magnificent Experimenter
Resulting in the Formation of the multitude
Of brilliant masses and formations in the many Heavens.

The vast variations of Beauty and the never ending displays
Within the total design of Controlled composition, were the Wonders
That only the Almighty, through the Mind of God and Eye of God,
Could Assemble, with the force.

And
The Creations
Were always Changing
Into new Displotions of Resplendence.

In Contrast, Spirits, once their nature was Formed,
Only each Being, by itself, was Given the Grace of God to Change.
The Maker Could Revise the nature of a Being,
But He did Not.

Now the Creator's Perception
Of the nature of Newness was Immense in Range in His Thoughts.
But the enigma of the Souls
Had Amplified His Emotion of Caution.

He was Not entirely Pleased
With the Souls' free will and free Spirit,
Yet He Enjoyed
The Originality of their ways.

Earth
Because of the past difficulties with the Roaming and Disruptive Souls,
The Creator Planned to Limit the Newness
To an area all of its own—
Especially to Restrict it from the Darkness of the Void.

God, El, was Aware of the Change in the nature of the Souls
Who had Passed Into the Chaos,
And He Wished Not any such possibility
With the Newness.

The Almighty did Not Wish
That there be any Chance
Of the Contamination of the Seventh Heaven
Of anything that was Not Known.

The First, Second, Fourth and Fifth Heavens were Not Proper.
The Sixth Heaven was too close to the Seventh.
Therefore,
He Chose the Third Heaven.

He Selected a small unhardened mass in a well Formed Galaxy
And Set Into Motion the Complex He Desired.
The mass that He Chose
Was Composed of all the elements that He Desired to Form His Newness.

Even in Relationship to its Galaxy it was Minute in size
For the Creator Wished to Keep His Newness very Confined.
It would Not be free in the Heavens,
As were the Spirits,

But Restrained, as other Elements
Within the limit of the pull of the Energy of the mass,
From the Allocation of the force, as were all other things subjected.
The mass had been Designated in the Book of Ashkish Records as (Earth).

The Newness Conceived[20]
Then through the Mind of God and the Eye of God, with the force,
Was Formed a Newness, that though of things, it Lived,
And it was different.
The Creator Called it Life. But it was Not with Spirit.

And from the elements of Earth,
God Caused the Formation of multiple myriads of Life.
And they Swirled among the gases and the liquids
On the surface of the Earth.

Now as Time went by,
The Almighty was both Pleased and Displeased.
He was Satisfied with the Making of something new,
But Not Filled with Joy at what was Formed.

For Life was Swept along among the vapors of the Earth
And at its Creation, because it was new and different,
God, El, had Decided that in its original nature it was to Continue
Only a period of Time and then Return to its original things.

Thus,
With the force,
Through the Mind of God and the Eye of God,
The Creator was Perpetually Replacing the Deceased Life.

Until the Formation of Life,
All the Spirits
Were Not Aware of Time
As being Important.

Time was Used as a Relationship
In the Harmonious Makeup of the World—
The Formations, the Sounds, the Beauties
The movement of the Time of Light into the Void.

Things were Limited in Time for Change,
But Spirit Life
Was Forever
In the TIME of the I AM.

The new Life was Not as Spirit
But of things
And it was Limited in its Lifetime,
Time took on new meaning to Spirit Beings.

Life Is Formed That Reproduces
And as Life, that had been Produced, Disintegrated
Into that with which it had been Composed,
The Thought of the Creator Centered Upon the Idea of the Strain of Life
That would be able to Conceive from itself another of like nature.

It would Propagate itself
In its own nature
Before it Disintegrated
Into its original composition.

The Vision of the Almighty's Contemplation
Was Tangent to the Creation of the Spirit Beings.
He had Brought About the Phenomena
Of the Division of His Original Self to Produce another.

The Conception of the new Strain of Life
Was Perceived
In Relation to the Separation of the Primary Spirit of God, El,
Into that of the Holy Spirit and Angels.

Then God, El, Caused the Strand of Life
To Absorb the Elements, Divide, and Form another
Of mass Image of themselves—
Though each new Strand was slightly Unique.

And All in the Heavens,
But the Holy Spirit and the Amilous who Understood,
Were Amazed
With Life being Able to Duplicate Variations of itself.

For ever before,
Only God, El,
With the force
Was Able to Create any thing or Being.

And All wondered about the Newness—
Especially Bael
Who Watched the new Principles of Life with Unusual Scrutiny—
Even for him.

Now,
The new Separations of the Strands of Life
Were Not Sufficient for the Omniscient One,
For each was only slightly different than the other.

Then,
The Maker Changed the Earth into a more Coagulated mass
With its surface continuously heated
By the fulminating Light from the great Galaxy.

And then,
From the Thought about the Formation of the Trinity
Came, from the Mind of God,
The Conception of the Coils of Life.

Two Strands of Life
Would Coil together,
Mix, Absorb the Elements, Divide and Form another
In the Combination of the two Donating Coils of Life—

As was the Spirit of the Amilous
The Result of the Lord God and the Holy Spirit
And as were the Souls
From the Amilous and the Angels.

But the Coils of Life were to be different from that of the Spirit Beings.
The new Life was to be Given the Memory of the Ability to Reproduce
    itself,
With each new Life Unique in itself,
As its own unit.

Then God, El, Placed the Coils of Life
In the liquid elements of the Earth
And they were Caused to Reproduce by the Memory within them-
    selves—
After a Predestined Growth.

Growth in size
Was different from Spirit Beings.
Souls and Angels were Surprised,
For they only Expanded in Emotions.

God Enjoyed His new Creations of Life
As it Spread Upon the Liquids of the Earth.
But each new Life was again Similar to the other
And their Beauty was Monotonous to the Creator.

The Spectacular Formations in the Heavens
Caused the Great Spirit, Maker, El,
To Desire a similar Display of Newness
On the Earth.

Nature of the Mind and Eyes of Spirits
Now the Nature of the Minds and Eyes
Of the Holy Spirit, the Amilous and all other Spirit Beings
Was an integral part of their Spirit,
With Emotional Harmony through the Mind of God and the Eye of God.

The Nature of the Mind of God and the Eye of God,
And their exact relationship with the Great Spirit,
Was Not Known by any
But the Almighty.

All Spirit Beings
But the Souls—
Were Attuned to the Mind of God and the Eye of God.
And Souls could become Attuned.

Thus the Thought and Feelings
Of the Holy Spirit, the Amilous and all other Beings
Were Noted
By the Mind of God and the Eye of God.

And with Concentration
The Spirit Beings
Could Utilize
The Great Mind of God and Eye of God.

Since their Formation,
The Holy Spirit and the Amilous,
Both were Cognizant of all that was Made
And nothing was made without their Knowledge.

Inspiration of the Holy Spirit—Water
The Holy Spirit Realized that God was Not Entirely Pleased with Life.
And the Holy One Thought upon this.
It had been the Imagination of the Holy Spirit
That had Given God the Amilous.

Once again the Holy Spirit Reflected upon the Creation of Life by God
And all His other Originations.
The Holy Spirit Knew that the Spirit Beings Increased,
With their Development of Emotions and Knowledge, by their Intensity.

The Thought of the Holy Spirit was that by Transposing this
To the things of Life through the purest of liquids—water—
That it could be Utilized to Renew the elements of Life,
Replacing the new and Ridding of the old would Develop better Life.

It was Not the only way to Develop Life
But it was a most Perfect way,
For God Perceived the Units of Life Forming together as one
Each with the Knowledge of the other.

The elements in Life Mixed with water
And new Strains Formed and Grew.
And as God Desired, they became more Beautiful as they Spread
About the warmed surface of the Earth.

Then God Attested to All,
"Henceforth, water and the Holy Spirit
Shall be thought of
As Generation of the Growth of Life."

"And the Blessing of water shall be Known to Life
Through the Holy One.
Life shall be Inspired and Blossom Forth with both.
And Life shall be Blessed with water."[21]

And the Earth was Caused to be Spread with water.
And All in the many Heavens were Pleased—Even Bael,
For part of him had come from the Holy One
And the Amilous had Not thought of it.

Early Life Survives
Some early Life Forms
Began to Mix with those with the Coils of Life
And Survived by Using the elements of the Newer Life.
And God did Not Change it.

The Maker Becomes Enamored with Life
Similar to the Creations
Of the Masses in the Heavens,
The Almighty Concentrated
Upon the Formation of Life on the Earth.

As the heat of the Light from the Galaxy Came Upon the water,
It began to Divide from the surface of the Earth into a mist.
With Life,
The land and rocks began to Appear.

And with the Energy of the Light
The Creator began to Change its Use
Into the Formation of even more Unique Life,
That Grew upon the Land.

Units with Coils of Life Flourished into Unusual Formations,
That Made the tiny planet, Earth,
Into a Magnificence
That Enhanced its Fascination by the many Spirit Beings.

The Divisions of Life
Then,
Through the Mind of God and the Eye of God,
Came to the Creator,
An even more pre-eminent Abstraction.

The New Life,
As were the First of the Lives,
Was Subjected
To its environment.

It was Not Able to Transfer itself from place to place
Except by the Impulse of its Surroundings
Or its Direction
Or Method of Growth.

The Innovative Thought of God
Was a different Succession of Life,
That could Move About the face of the Earth
As the Spirit Beings did in the Heavens.

Again,
Because the New Variation of Life was an unknown,
The Creator would Start it relatively small to the Earth
And it would Return to the elements in a short span of Time.

Then God
Designated the First Lives, Planal,
The First Coils of Life Creation He Called Plant
And the New Variation He Named Animal.

The Difference of Animal Life
Now,
Of All that had ever been Made,
The Animal
Developed in a different manner.

The Planal to Survive, had Formed with other Life.
But this new Variation of Life Forced the Sacrifice of Plants—
As well as other Animals—
And Absorbed them for its Maintenance and Growth.

It was Reluctant
To Sacrifice itself for others.
Animal Utilized all
For its own selfish Preservation.

All the Beings in the Heavens
Were Surprised
At this major Deviation of Living things—
But Bael was Fascinated.

Separation of Waters–
Blood by the Amilous Causes Growth of Animals
Much Time Passed
From the Formation
Of Planal and Plant Life on the Ocean surface,
Until the Thought of Animal Life.

During this Time
The mist of waters,
That Rose above the Earth,
Separated even more.

The Absorption of the Light Energy by the Plants
Caused many of the Elements,
That were Discarded by them,
To Rise into the air—with the mists of water.

Then God Caused
The Separation of the elements of the water of the mists
From the elements and water on the surface of the Earth.
And it was as a Shield from many of the rays of Light.

Then the Animal Life
Responded to the Lessening of Light waves on the Land
And they began to Move upon it
And their Units began to Grow.

Now,
During the Formation of Life on Earth,
All the Heavenly Beings
Concentrated on the Newness.

But,
Only the Holy Spirit, the Amilous—and Bael, Michael and Belzebel—
Observed the actual Process
Of the Development of Life.

The Holy Spirit did so because of Concern, the Amilous because of
    Renewal,
Michael and Belzebel from their innate curiosity—
But for Bael, he Hoped to find a way
To Show the Almighty his Expanding Knowledge.

Bael Believed
He could Prove
He was Capable of Controlling the Future
Better than the Amilous.

But then the Amilous,
Remembering the water of the Holy Spirit,
Conceived the Thought of blood
To Expand the Growth of Animals.

And from the Mind of God and the Eye of God,
The Creator Caused Life on Earth
To Feel more of the Vibrations of the Heavens.
And Life Grew.

Then from the blood
The Units of Life Generated the most efficient of Animal Life.
And the (worm)
Became the basis of those of blood.

Then was Conceived the first Magnificent Creatures that Developed
    hardness,
Some within their bodies and some outside,
From the Advent of the blood.
And they Swam the oceans and then Walked the lands.

And God Conveyed to All,
"Surely the Amilous is the True Son of God, the Keeper of THE WORD,
And as the First Son of God will Inherit
The World of the I AM THAT I AM."

And All in the Heavens were Pleased—
Except Bael,
Who was Furious and Sulked.
And God Knew.

Uniqueness of Things, Spirit Beings and Life

God Willed that All in the I AM Not to be the same,
Every thing, Mass, Galaxy, Universe, Heaven,
All Spirit Beings and all Life were Not alike—
Even if minutely.

All things continuously Changed,
Though the force, with the Ever-Expanding Imagination of God.
This was true of the smallest of things
In the vast Heavens of the I AM.

Spirit Beings—
Because their nature and essence were pure Thought—
Only Altered
With the Advancement of Emotions and Knowledge.

Heavenly Beings were Not Subjected to the Time of Light
In Traversing the many Heavens,
But Transported themselves by Desire—
As did God.

But
The nature of the Creator of the I AM
Was
That He was Everywhere.

However, the Concentration of the Almighty,
Through the Mind of God and the Eye of Cod,
Moved forever
Within the I AM.

Even then
The Omniscient One was Aware at all times of All within the I AM
And All with him—
With the exception of the Souls.

For the Souls
Were once removed from the Creator
At their Inception—
Being from the Amilous and the Angels.

It took the Concentration of God
Or the Soul
To Make
A pure Awareness.

The Almighty was Cognizant of their place in the Heavens,
For they were of Essence,
And their Thoughts Came Into His Conscious,
But Not always His into the Souls.

Thus,
The Souls
Moved with free will,
Their lack of pure Cohesion with God,

At times,
Confused their Thought process
And Left them Entangled with the masses of the Heavens
And even amongst themselves.

But even then
The Infinite one did Not Change their Nature,
As He did Not deliberately Change any Spirit Being—
They Only Changed themselves.

Life was different.
It was Not of Spirit.
It was part of the I AM.
It was Made Up of things.

It Lived
And had Attunement with the I AM,
But Not
As did the Spirit Beings.

The basic nature
Of the Separate Forms of Life
Did Not Change
But could be Added to by the Creator.

Knowledge of Growth and Refinement
Was in the basic nature of Life,
But because they were of things, the Creator Altered and Adapted
Their Beings as they Developed in size and in numbers.

But each new Life Form was Divided from the others
And each Retained its nature
The Coils of Life Formed masses of Units
That Functioned as one.

The offspring of the Coils
Became the New and Dominant parts of the Coils
And Made each new Life Unique.
Their Adaptation to their Surrounding was Carried to the New.

And they Evolved
With Knowledge in their Coils
To Create within themselves Newness
And the Creator could Add to this Knowledge.

Spirit Beings were Able, by the Grace of God,
Through the Mind of God and the Eye of God,
To Enjoy all of the Vibrations of the Heavens—
Its Harmony and Beauty—as did the Almighty.

And with the Creator,
Life began to Adapt their parts to Know these Vibrations
Through feel, smell, sound and sight—
Especially the Creatures.

These were the Transpositions
From those of Spirit to those of Life,
With the Grace of God.
And God was Pleased with Life.

But of All that Lived,
One Characteristic of Animal Life was the most Divergent.
Except for its offspring—and then Not always—
Few in the Animal Life Sacrificed for others—until its Death.

As Plant Life, the most adaptable Survived,
But Animal Life did so by Forcing the Sacrifice of Plant Life
And other Animal Life—
As well as Absorbing the elements they needed.

Thus in All of the I AM
This nature of Animals
Was Foreign
To that of other Creations of the Almighty

It was strange
To the greatest law of God
The Sacrifice
Of One for Another.

Sacrifice had always been the Ultimate of Love,
And which until then,
Had Controlled the Emotions and Knowledge of All
In the I AM.

This Change
Caused all Being
To Contemplate its Meaning—
And Intrigued Bael.

Bael Notices the Coils of Life Can Change
Now Bael became Aware that the Coils of Life could be changed—
Through the Thrust with the force, by God, by Adaptation to the envi-
    ronment
Or even Disorientation by great upheavals
And Catastrophes of wandering fragments of the Universe.

It was Then that Bael Asked God
To be Allowed, to Utilize his Knowledge
To Further the Development of a Creature
That had Not been Known Before.

Now God Knew
Of the great Desire of Bael
To Please Him
And He Granted his Request.

Then through the Mind of God and the Eye of God, with the force,
The Creator in Attunement with the Thoughts of Bael
Caused a Creature Insect to Develop Wings
And it Flew in the air above the surface of the Earth.

And Bael Called it (Fly).
Now All in the Heavens were in Wonder at this Deed,
For until then,
Only the Holy Spirit and the Amilous Aided in any Creation.

Bael Aids in Creation And Is Made Master of the Reptiles
Now Bael
Had Particularly Noticed those Creatures
That Moved from the Oceans to the Land
And lived in both

He Saw that many had Grown in great size
In comparison to the other Animals.
And Bael became Fascinated with these Creatures
That were so much larger than the rest.

Then Bael again Asked God to let him Develop new Creatures.
But Further he Requested to be Granted a limited Use of the force
To Manipulate the Coils of Life
To Create his own Creatures.

Now Never before had any Being Asked for such Power
And all were Astonished.
Now even God had been Satisfied with the Creation of the (Fly),
For it was indeed a great Newness.

Then God Granted the great last formed Archangel his Petition.
Then Bael began to Form
Those that he Called (Reptiles)
And Further Develop Winged Insects and Creatures.

The Beings in the Heavens were both Surprised and Happy
With Bael's new interest, for they wished for some Diversion
That would keep the last Formed Archangel from Tormenting the Souls
And his Disturbing many of the Angels—and the Amilous.

Now the Almighty
Also was Cognizant
Of the close Relationship of Michael and Belzebel to Bael
And their knowledge of Life.

Then He Gave similar Authority to Belzebel
Of all life that was in the Seas
And to Michael all Life on Land
But the Reptiles—and the insects.

But they and all on the Earth
Were Subject to God and the Trinity.
Thus Began the Sovereignty over Life
By other than God.

Bael Takes the Earthly Shape of a Serpent
Bael was very Serious about his Power over the Reptiles—and Insects.
He was thoroughly familiar with the use of the Coils of Life.
He Directed the Breeding of the Reptiles
So that Compared to other of the major Creatures they were vast

In number, size and became in control of all about them
And their environment—some even to flight.
Compared to Baels',
Michaels' and Belzebels' Adaptations were of minor consequence.

Bael became so Enamored with his Abilities
To Produce such Dominating strains in relation to other Life,
That he found himself Desiring to Project himself into an Earthly Form
So that he could be Recognized by them.

Their only Knowledge of him was through Thought Transference.
Bael had Scrutinized the Characteristics of the Materiality of Life.
He Knew the Essence of Spirit was different
Than the Substance of Life.

A thing was Formed by the Reduction of Light of the I AM.
But the Essence of Spirit was Unique,
For its Propulsion was Above the Light.
It was Pure Light.

But Bael Reasoned that by Thought
He could Reverse his Pure Light Essence
Entirely through that of Light
And Into Matter.

Then through his Concentration, Bael Compressed himself,
With his little Knowledge of the Use of the force,
Within a huge hollow in the Bowels of the Earth
And Made himself into a grotesque Serpent-like Being.

For he was at first
Not Able to Control his shape.
Only Michael, Belzebel—God and the Trinity—
Knew what he had done.

Since the Appearance that Bael became
Was from the Projection of Thought and Not from the Coils of Life,
He was Able to Conjure Up, with minor Use of the force,
Figures Never Before Observed.

From his original Serpent-like Being,
He Changed his features in a thousand ways—
Adding gigantic wings, protruding horns, giant genitals
Strange heads, unusual tails, slippery and scaly bodies.

But each Guise
Was Intended to Convey
That he was the master of the Reptilians and all that flew.
And God became Aware.

Now God was Not Pleased—
For He was the Creator.
And Bael had Used the force for something Above
What the Almighty had Intended.

God Creates Glorious Earthly Thought Forms
The Great Spirit, El, Realized that Michael
Could Not Resist a similar experience to Make an Earthly Form.
Then the Creator Sent a Vision of Marvelous Creature Beauty
Through the Thoughts of the Almighty's favorite Archangel, Michael.

Then Michael,
Using what he Knew of the force,
Transposed himself into a Magnificent Pure Radiantly White Figure
With a gigantic set of wings.

Michael's entire Presence
Was the Configuration
Which the Creator Wished an Archangel to Resemble.
And, as Bael, he could Form with or without wings.

The Ever Wavering Belzebel, in Attempting to Duplicate a Shape
Similar but different from his Companions,
Could do nothing but Mix into a half Composition Amphibian
To Show his Domination of the Seas.

The other part of him was like that of Michael
And of great Beauty,
But even then his Attempt to Duplicate Wings
Resulted in Resemblance of fish fins.

But the Feat of the trio was that for the first time,
Thought Creatures were Constructed.
Before this
No solid Beings had Come From other than the Creations of Life.

So it came to pass,
Configurations had come from Thought
And the original Use of the force
By the Shrewd and Brilliant Bael.

God Pondered such Happenings
By other than Himself.
He Gave Contemplation to the Problems that might occur
In the future.

He was Not Happy with the Forms of Bael and Belzebel
For other of the Heavenly Beings—
Either their Original Shapes or those they Changed into
By their Thoughts.

The Almighty's Decision was Major and Momentous.
The Amilous, the other Archangels and the Angels
Received from the Creator a Vision of Earthly Forms
That they would Assume if they Appeared Upon the Earth.

Since they were Thought Forms
They could be Changed by God.
Only the Holy Spirit and the Souls
Remained without Knowledge of Earthly Shapes.

The Holy Spirit was Not Shown because God did Not Desire it
And the Souls could Not because they were too shallow of Essence,
    Unstable
And Not totally Attuned to God
To Attain Perfection.

Now
The Almighty
Did Not Make Himself into a Form,
For He was too Vast.

But with the Part of Him
That was the Lord God
He Created A Superb Physique and a Magnificent Physiognomy
That was Superior to All others.

And He Presented Himself
So that All could See.
In the Lord God, the Great Spirit, El,
Presented the Perfect Earthly Creature Creation.

And even Bael was
Overwhelmed by Lord God's Brilliance.
Bael also Misunderstood
The Motives of the Almighty,

For he Assumed
That the Creator was Elated with his Conversion from Pure Spirit
To that of Earthly mass Form—
Though God did Not Indicate this to Bael.

But Bael Saw the Lord God in His Magnificent Earthly Form—
And all those of the Amilous, Archangels and Angels—
And Believed his Thought Formation to be equally as Marvelous
As the water of the Holy Spirit and the blood of the Amilous.

Then God Created the Thought Form of Bael
That He desired Bael to have.
And it was a Brilliance.
That Equaled Michael's.

Bael could Choose his form
His own Creation
Or that of God, El.
And All in the Heavens Marveled at this.

Then, God Commanded
That None but Bael, Michael and Belzebel
With their Thought Forms
Could come upon the Earth.

Bael's Reptiles Dominate the Earth
Now as much time Passed,
Bael, Michael and Belzebel, with their Limited Use of the force,
Mated Unusual strains of the Coils of Life in Plants and Animals
On Land, Seas and those Amphibians.

Bael had been the most Perceptive
And also the one with the most Desire to Outstrip his Comrades.
And with his Use of the force, Bael Wove the Coils of Life so that
Monsters were Produced that Dominated all of the other Creatures

And the Reptiles began to Destroy
All other of Flesh
And to Monopolize the Vegetation
Of the Earth.

Bael Defies God
Then God Requested
That Bael Restrain those in his Domain.
And Bael, who had Desired Praise for his Achievement, Sulked
And Refused.

In All the Time of the I AM
No Heavenly Being or thing
Had ever Not Obeyed
A Direct Order of the Almighty.

Then the Omnipotent One,
To Show Physical Power Against the Physical Creatures of Bael,
Sent huge fire-balls, Trailing toxic gaseous elements
About the upper surface of the Earth.

And the toxic elements,
Mixed with the Life Sustaining Atmosphere
Became Compressed by the fire-balls
Into a thin layer about the Earth.

And the Earth
Was Caused to Turn
From the Pull
Of the Circling masses.

Only the smaller Animals, those Shielded by rocks or caves,
Those beneath the waters, those at the ends of the planet,
Only those Lived—as did the Plants that were Sheltered.
But the large Reptiles of Bael were nearly Obliterated.

Then, as the Earth Turned
From the great Pull of the fire-balls,
The Death Dealing vapors were gone.
And Bael was cast into the Abyss.

All the Beings
Were Mute with Terror
At this Display of Vengeance
By the God of the I AM.

Realignment of the Archangels
Never in His TIME had God been more Disturbed.
Yet the Omniscient One Understood the Frustrations of Bael
For He Knew much was the Love of Bael for Himself that had Caused
The Problems that Arose from the Creation of the Reptiles.

He Knew, however,
That Bael's Defiance could Not go without Punishment,
But God did Not Wish to Curb the extraordinary Skills and Knowledge
Of the last Formed Archangel.

Then the Almighty Conveyed to All,
"Henceforth, Bael may Not Come Upon the Earth!
But Bael shall have Dominion over the First Heaven!
And he shall be known as the King of the First Heaven!"

Now the Amilous
Did Not Understand
And for the first time
He was Not in Accord with the Omniscient One.

Then the Great Spirit El,
Made Known to the Amilous and All in the Heavens,
"The Amilous shall be with Me
Until the End of ALL TIME.

But the Return of one Errant Being to the Heavens
Is Cause for Great Joy."
And great was the Pleasure of the Amilous
At this Knowledge.

Bael Becomes Ruler of the Fiery Heaven
Now All Knew the Tribulations of the First Heaven.
It was the Incandescent Beginning of the I AM
From that which WAS.
Its State was Pure White Light.

The Fiery Radiance was such
That only the Almighty had,
In Time Past,
Been Able to Mingle In Its Center.

The Holy Spirit and the Amilous
Spent much Time there
For its Purifying Effect Upon the Emotions—
Especially Developing those of Love.

Many were the Souls
That Spent unwanted periods at its edges
To Bathe in the Purifying Light
For their misdeeds.

Thus the Transposition of Bael to the First Heaven
Was of two-fold purpose—
To Remove him from any Influence on the Earth with its Life
And to Realign his Warped Emotions and Knowledge.

All the Beings in the Heavens
Were Awed
At Bael's Task
Of having Power over the Fearsome First Heaven.

And Bael Took his new Duty with great pride and Joy,
For he Thought
Only he—and God—
Could Handle the Fiery Cradle of the I AM.

Bael Surmised that it was the Almighty's way to Test him,
For in this way God could find if he could control the Renewal
At the Time
Of the End of the I AM.

No longer did Bael Resent
The Major Demise of most of the Reptiles he had Developed,
For he Felt it was their Ascendancy Upon the Earth
That had Shown God Proof of his Abilities and his great Knowledge.

And God Knew and was Not Pleased.
Then, so it would be Known by all
That the new Assignment for Bael
Was Not a Reward for his Disobedience,

God Conveyed,
"Henceforth,
Subject to the Almighty and the Trinity,
Each Archangel shall be charged with a Heaven.

Belzebel shall have the Second Heaven,
Michael the Third Heaven,
Gabriel the Fourth
Baraqiel the Fifth, Raphael the Sixth.

The One with the most Organized Thinking, Uriel, shall Command,
Directly Subject to the Lord God, the Holy One and the Amilous,
The Seventh Heaven. And Uriel shall be directly Aided by The Metatron,
The Sandalphon and all the Heads of Angels.

And each Chief of Angels of each Heaven,
Shall be Subject to their Archangel. And all Archangels shall be
Further Guided in the Use of the force, to Harmonize all in their care,
With the Almighty God, Creator of All in the I AM."

The Changes on Earth
Following the Destruction of much of Earth's Life,
The variety and expanse of Vegetation,
At first,
Developed much more rapidly than did Animal Life.

This Brought About an elemental difference of the air
Near the surface of the Earth.
The Days of Light, that Came Upon the Earth from the Galaxy,
Were Refracted and the land Cooled, especially near its fringes,

This Change
Brought much more rapidly than before
And new species of Plants and Creatures Came Upon the Earth
To Cope with the new environment.

And God was Pleased
With the Change,
For the Supremacy of Bael's Reptiles
Was over.

Souls Enter Creatures
At first
Michael was very Enthusiastic with his new Command of the Third
    Heaven.
And he Spread his Time in Developing and Maintaining the Harmony
Of all of the Heaven and the Earth.

With Bael gone,
The Souls began Hovering about the Third Heaven
And Taunting their Beloved Archangel, Michael,
Into Adventures.

At first,
He was Irritated by their Boisterousness.
But as the newness of his Assignment Wore Off,
He Started to become more Enthusiastic about their Impetuous nature.

The Souls Tried to Disrupt the Harmony of the Third Heaven,
But Michael,
With a slight Use of the force,
Found he could Control them more than ever before.

Soon
The Souls Grew Tired and Frustrated
At Michael's Ability
To Thwart their Attempts to Disrupt him.

So with the great Reduction of Bael's Reptiles on the Earth,
The playful Souls
Began Hovering about the Earth
To see what mischief they could find.

Now the Souls had the Ability to Enter into masses
By Condensing their Spirit Essence
And they Discovered they could Slip into those on Earth.
But it was the Creatures that they found exciting.

They Ascertained
They could Guide the Animals
Causing them to Show Competence Not before Demonstrated.
This was especially true of the newer large Animals.

And the Souls Deceived Michael with such grand Illusion,
That the First Formed Archangel Rushed to Tell Bael and Belzebel,
In their Heavens,
Of his Development of those large Beasts.

Now Bael could Not Come Upon the Earth,
But it took him only a brief time
To Comprehend
What the Souls had done.

And Belzebel,
Himself a Master of Deceit,
Was Uproarious with Delight and Satisfaction at what had Transpired,
For the lowly Souls had Outwitted the Magnificent Michael.

Belzebel Knew that both Michael and Bael
Looked Upon him as less Competent than themselves.
This Successful Ruse upon Michael
By the far less intelligent Souls, was a great Joy to Belzebel.

And he Conveyed the Event
With great Humor to All the Beings in the Heavens.
But Michael took it Jovially and it was soon Forgotten,
But by God and the Trinity—and Bael.

Those Souls Involved had Expected to be Punished
By Being Sent to Bael
For Purification in the White Light of the First Heaven.
But neither Michael or God did so.

But for a long period of Time
The Souls did Not Entangle themselves into the Beasts
And even Avoided the Third Heaven
To be with the Amilous in the Seventh Heaven.

For
Many New and Exciting Events
Were Happening
There.

The Lord God and the Seventh Heaven
The Projection of the Lord God was such
That though there was Not Separation from the Almighty God, El,
The Ability to Make a Physical Form from Himself
Was a Unique Experience for the Creator.

The Holy Spirit and the Amilous
Were as Vines to the Trunk of the Light of the Great Spirit, El.
But the Lord God
Was of the Trunk of the Pure Light of God.

The Mystery of the Great Spirit
Was to be in All Places of the I AM without Separation,
But to Control All, with the force,
As if He were.

Thus that Part of the Almighty that was the Lord God—
Though Not Divided—
Acted Individually,
And yet did Not.

The Lord God was a Share of the Trinity
With the Holy One and the Amilous
Who were as One,
Yet they were Not.

God, El, the Father Creator of All Beings,
Was Not as One with the Trinity,
But the Lord God
Was with God as One—

And also One with the Trinity—
Though the Almighty, El, was Not,
The Lord God was of the Spirit of the Almighty
But also could Incarnate a Physical Form.

In no other place but Earth
Had there been any Form that Lived.
But the Seventh Heaven
Had been Designated as the Place of the Lord God.

Then on a Coagulated mass that far Overshadowed that of Earth,
The Creator through the Lord God,
With the Mind of God and the Eye of God, with the force,
Fashioned a Place of Physical Beauty in the Seventh Heaven.

It was Re-formed
With high mountains of lands with vast areas of valleys
And waters
As pure as the Holy Spirit.

It was Warmed by Light
But its Magnificence
Was Enhanced by huge structures of ice crystals.
And the Lord God Called it Kingdom.

Now there was vegetation
And Creatures Formed
But they did Not Expand, but Changed
And they did Not Die.

Each group was New and Defined.
No creature was as the Reptiles.
Those that Resembled the large Plants of Earth
Were of a Fragrance Not Known on the Planet of Life.

And the Aroma from them, the Special Herbs and the Trees of Life,
With the Fruits from the Trees of Life
And the water Pure of salt,
Sustained the Physical Forms of the Heavenly Beings.

And there was little salt upon the Planet of the Lord,
For Incarnated Beings of Heaven
Were Physically affected by too much salt,
Disintegrating their Structure.

The Heavenly Beings' Manner was the same
In the Kingdom of Lord God as they were on Earth
And their Shapes were as those
That had been Pre-conceived by God, El.

All was Made Whole, by the force,
As Imaged with the Thoughts of the Lord God
Thus All in the Kingdom were Pure in their Composition and Nature,
And Not Subject to error as were the Coils of Life.

Because of their nature
It was Not necessary for Creatures and other Organisms of the Kingdom
To Sacrifice for others.
The Kingdom of the Lord God was Peaceful.

Then the Lord God
Formed a Magnificent Structure
In the form of that of the Ashkish.
That contained the Book of Records.

It was a Splendid Pyramid
Of multi-colored stones
Inlaid with the Purest of Gold
And Precious Stones.

And He Made an Elegant Throne of Gold and Stones of Brilliance
In His Throne Room that was Inlaid
With Gold, Gems and other Splendid Minor masses of things
That were Created while God was Forming the Seventh Heaven.

And when the Lord God Sat Upon the Throne,
The Almighty Called Him King of His Kingdom.
Then an Adorned Throne Seat
Was Set on the Right Hand of the Lord for the Amilous

And a Similar Chair to his left
That was Reserved for the Holy One
Who was Not yet
In Incarnate Form.

And The Metatron and Sandalphon,
The first Formed Angels,
Sat in the Back, Not Above Him,
To Maintain the Court of Angels.

And the Archangel, Uriel,
Ruled the Heads of the Angels of the Seventh Heaven—
Sammael, Head of the Seraphim;
Ophaniel, Head of the Cherubim;

Zaphkiel, Head of the Thrones;
Anaphiel, Head of the Crowns;
Chief Ariel of the Potentates,
Who also Governed the Thrones and Crowns.

And through this Hierarchy
A Vast Array of Angels
Did the Bidding
Of the Lord God.

And in this Court the Lord God and his Twelve—
The Metatron or Sandalphon
And the Eleven Heads and Chiefs of Angels—
Settled Disputes among the Angels.

Thus
The Kingdom of the Lord God
Was Vastly different
Than was on Earth.

But once Again
The Souls were Not Able to Form on the Kingdom of the Lord
For the same Reason they had Not been Able to on Earth—
Their Essence was too Infirm to Materialize.

The D-Evil Uses Force to Punish
The Formation of the Kingdom of the Lord God did Not Disturb Bael.
But the Placing of the Incarnated Amilous
At the Right Hand of the Throne
Infuriated the Shrewd and Last Created Archangel.

Bael then Converged his Entire Energy
Upon the Knowledge he had of the force
And of the Pure White Light
Of the First Heaven.

Unlike All other Spirits,
Whose Motivation for Entering the Pure White Light
Was the Absorption of Purity and Love,
Bael's Concern was to Realign the Heaven

For the Wonderment of the Almighty
So that He might Choose him to be the Deity of the Renewal—
Instead of the Amilous.
Thus Bael Focused on that which was the Center of All the World.

Also, through Knowledgeable Experimentation,
Bael Devised Methods of Torment, Unknown until then
To be Used Upon the Errant Souls
Before they were Allowed Into the Purifying White Light.

They became Fearful of Bael and for a while they Avoided,
When possible, the Disturbing of the Heavens.
But soon they Returned to their Impulsive Ways
And were Punished.

The Mischievous Souls
Began to Call
The Misdeeds that they Committed
By the name of Evil.

Bael, who Meted Out the Manner of Contrition
Before the Purification in the Pure White Light
Was Aptly Named the Dispenser of Evil Punishment—
Or simply—the D-Evil.

That Area
That Bael Used for his Torments
Was Named Hell.
And Bael Enjoyed the new Titles.

Now God was neither Pleased or Displeased—
For though there was Resentment among those Chastised,
There was Also a Remarkable Improvement
In the Soul's Disruption of the Heavens.

And,
Except for those Unfortunates
That Came Into the Second Heaven of Belzebel,
Fewer Souls Appeared before Bael.

But Belzebel Enjoyed Observing the Agony of the Errant Souls,
And found Ways to Encourage their Waywardness.
But those that Came Unto Bael the Most,
Were Those Souls that had previously Wandered into the Void.

Their Emotions sometimes Appeared Warped and even Out of Control.
There was little that Passed the Scrutiny of the Shrewd Last Archangel
And Bael became very Cognitive of the Infirmity of these Souls.
As did God.

Michael Is Lonely
It was Michael who Found
The Creation of the Kingdom of the Lord God and Alienation.
For Michael Lost the Company of the ever Roving Souls
Who were Attracted to the Newness of the Seventh Heaven.

The Staidness of the Angels in his Third Heaven
Gave him little true Fellowship.
The Pleasures of the Seventh Heaven
Did Not Filter Down to Michael's Third Heaven.

He Missed the Stimulation of Bael
And even the Strangeness of Belzebel.
Then Michael began to Roam
And Visit the Spirits of Bael and Belzebel.

The First Heaven was Overwhelming,
Even for Bael.
He was Not sure how to Handle
The Fiery White Light.

His only Diversion
Was his Unique Modes of the Chastising
Of those Souls
Who Strayed from the Way of God.

His Focusing
Upon the Project of the Incandescent Cradle of the I AM
Gave him little Incentive
To Fraternize with Michael and Belzebel.

He also
Feared Going near the Earth,
As God
Had Forbidden his being upon it.

Michael Found the First Heaven to be Infectious
With its Illuminating Pure White Light,
Which was Different than Light.
For it was the Perfect Projection of that which WAS.

But Michael was Adverse
To Watching the Castigation
Of those Souls
Who had been Sent to Bael.

The Second Heaven,
Ruled by Belzebel,
Was almost entirely Devoid of Solid Masses of any size.
Its State was nearly without elements but one.

Its Vacuum-like Condition
Was such
That it Shielded the Third Heaven and other Heavens
From the Intensity of the First Heaven.

And Created a Perfect Constant Restraint
Upon the Outward Movement
Of the other Heavens
And All Within them.

It was the Second Heaven
That would Draw Inward the I AM at its End, with the force.
The Second Heaven was a Place
With which Belzebel Knew Not what to Do.

Thus Belzebel began Returning to Earth and the lonely Michael.
Michael was Pleased—but he Missed the Stimulation of Bael.
After much Time had Passed,
The playful Michael had a Profound Thought.

Bael could Not Come Upon the Earth
Or Control anything Upon the Earth—
But God had Not Indicated that Bael
Could Not Go Beneath the Surface of the Earth.

The Almighty had Not Mentioned anything about Bael
Not Going Within the Earth
Or Not
Having any Authority there.

Under the Crust of the Land
Were Vast Caves and Total Inner Earth.
And Michael Explained his Perception to Bael and Belzebel.
They Contemplated Michael's Reasoning and Reservedly Agreed,

Now Michael
Was Not One to Disobey God,
But his Missing of Bael's Friendship
And his natural Mischievous Makeup,

He could Not Help but Interpret His Command
In a way that would Not Exactly or Totally Violate God's Decree,
But still Allow him to Exchange Abstract Thoughts and Knowledge
With his great Companion, Bael, within the area of the Earth.

Then the Adventurous Michael,
The Devious Belzebel and the Shrewd Bael,
Searched for giant Caves in the Underground
And Explored under the surface of the Earth—as did the Souls.

An Unexpected thing Happened.
The eggs of many of Bael's Reptiles
Were Found to have Survived
In the Caves.

But all Feared to Hatch them for they might Wander to the Land
Where Bael was to have no Control,
Even though many of the smaller Reptiles
Still Lived upon the Earth, they were Not Dominant.

Thus the Underground became a Place of Bael,
When he Left his First Heaven.
God Knew and was Annoyed, but did Not Interfere,
For He was Aware of Michael's Need for the Magnitude of Bael.

Souls Return to the Earth
The Realization that they Could Not have a Physical Existence
In the Kingdom of the Lord God
Renewed the Interest of the Souls
For the Creatures of the Earth.

Though the Souls
Could Not have a Corporeal Configuration upon the Earth,
They were Able to Enter the Flesh and Blood bodies
And Experience them almost as if they were their own.

Those that were Curiosity Seeking Souls
Enjoyed Particularly the Exhilaration of Creature Sexuality,
Plus the Chasing or Gathering of food
And the Pleasures of its Consumption.

The Difference of the Emotions of those of Flesh and Blood
In Regard to Feelings, Tastes, Smells and other Sensations
Brought more and more Souls
Into the great Beasts of the Earth.

The Amilous and the Holy Spirit were Not Happy
With this Tendency of the Frolicsome Souls
Or the Lightheartedness of Michael
Toward the Souls' Ventures.

But the Concentration of God, with the Lord God,
Upon the Kingdom,
Proved a Deterrent to any Action
Against the ways of those Errant Souls.

Souls Begin to Develop New Forms
Now as the Souls
Began to Enter into the Creatures,
They began to Desire Forms
Different from the Beasts of the Earth,

Though many
Were the Imaginations
Of the Souls that Came to Earth
About the Structure of Animal Forms,

There was a Predominant Aspiration by those Souls
To Develop Creatures
Into the Images of the Earthly Form of Angels
And as were Angels with the Kingdom of the Lord God.

And the Souls
Chose to Enter more and more
Those Creatures
That most Resembled the Likeness of the Angels.

Though Souls were Not Able to Manipulate the Coils of Life,
As did Bael,
They became aware that by Mating of Certain Creatures
And by Entering their unborn bodies

They were Able
With their Thoughts and Essence
To slightly Maneuver the Structure of the Beasts
Which Carried Over in the Memory of the Coils of Life.

This Brought About,
Over Periods of Time,
A Variety of Creatures that had the Upright Form of the Angels
But the Appearance of the Beasts.

Now
Before their Entry into the Creatures of Earth,
The Free Willed And Free Spirited Souls
Were Able to Develop their Thoughts.

But
When they became Enmeshed into the Beasts
They Found that Over Time,
They became Subject to the natural nature of the Animal they Entered

Until it Died
Or they Extricated themselves
And Returned
To their Spirit nature.

As the Souls Continued their Experiments
With the Advancement of Beasts,
They began to Succeed in the Development
Of the Structure of the Creatures' Capacity of Mind,

But
They were Unable to Change
The Animalistic nature
But a slight degree.

Now Souls were Not Male or Female as were the Creatures of Earth.
Souls Became as the Gender of the Animal they Entered.
But many Souls would Move from one Creature Sex to another
And they began to Enjoy Unorthodox Behavior.

The Great Spirit became Concerned
With those Activities of the Souls
And was Dismayed with their Quest
In the Evolvement of the Beasts of Earth

And
Their own Participation
In the Variety of pleasures
That they Discovered.

And the Creator again was Drawn to Concentrate upon the Earth.
From the Mind of God and the Eye of God
Came the Vision that would Change the Focus of All the Beings
Relating to the Earth.

All Life was Different from things and Spirit Beings.
Life although Made of elemental things,
Formed itself through the Coils of Life.
Life was Not Spirit, though it Lived as did Spirit.

But it Lived only a short span of Time
And Returned to the elements
By Sacrifice through direct Absorption by others or, at its Death,
It Returned to Earth for its Use in the Growth of others.

Then God Altered the Coils of Life in an Advanced Creature
To Form those which He Called Amen.
The Amen was Structured as the Primates
That the Souls had Caused to Develop.

But they more Resembled the Configuration of the heads of Angels
And they were Flesh and Blood
Their skin
Was more the smooth texture of Angels.[22]

Then He Entered into the Amen
Spirit from Himself
That took on the Dimensions and Shape of the Form of Amen—
Though it was Flexible and Not Confined to this outline.

The Spirit of Amen
Was Attached to it
With a direct source to its brain,
Which was Expanded.

The Amen's Spirit Knowledge and Emotions
That were Endowed by the Creator,
Were as One with that of the Flesh and Blood,
Though Separate.

The Creature Knowledge and Emotions
That Came from the Coils of Life
Were greatly Enhanced
By that of the Spirit.

Now Amens were Male and Female.
And their offspring Carried
In their Coils of Life
A Portion of the Parents' Spirit.

The new Amens' Spirit Emotions Grew as did the Body.
At the Death of the Amen the Flesh and Blood Returned to the Elements
And, but for that Part Passed in the Coils of Life,
The Spirit Returned to God.

Thus the Spirit of the Amen
Was Different,
For it Came
From the Coils of Life.

The Spirit Increased
And its Developed Spirit,
But for that Given to its Offspring,
Again Merged with the Creator.

Amens' Spirit
Was the first and only Spirit
That Restored itself
With the Great Spirit.

The Spirit of the Amens
Expanding in Pure, Loving and Reverent Emotions and Knowledge of God
And Reverting to the Almighty Spirit
Was most Pleasing to God.

Although they were Below the Heavenly Spirits,
Of all the Spirits,
With the Exception of the Holy Spirit and the Amilous,
That of the Amen was the most Gratifying to the Creator of All.

All the Heavenly Beings were Astonished
By the Earthly Spirits of Amens
And the Relationship
They had with God.

And
The Heavenly Spirits Longed to be
As the Amen—
But Bael and Belzebel.

Then because of the Purity of their Spirit,
Amens were put under the care of the Holy One,
With the Lord God and the Amilous,
To Assure this Continuity.

But Michael was Given the direct task of Overseeing the Amen—
As well as other Life—
For the Earth was in the Third Heaven,
Which was his Domain.

Michael's Frustration with Amens
Because the Species of Amen
Appeared upon the Earth
In such an Advance State of Knowledge and Emotions
Over all other Forms of Life,

The Gregarious Michael
Made great Effort to Develop them as Companion—
An association which he Missed so much with Bael—
And even the Devious Belzebel.

But the Flesh and Blood Incarnations of the Amen
Were quite limited
In their Comprehension of Michael's Heavenly Spirit Form
For they were only Attuned to God.

In their Earthly Composition,
The Amens were sore afraid of Michael,
Which led
To No close association.

So Michael Frustratedly Tried to Help them as he could,
And Spent his Time Keeping the rest of the Earth
And the Third Heaven
In its true relationship with Arrangements Desired by God.

Now the Souls
Became Aware
Of how Perturbed Michael was
With the Amen.

So they began Hovering around the Earth
And Entering more and more Primate Creatures
And Attempted to Compete with their Minds and in Actions
With the Amen.

But the Creatures Entered by Souls
And the Amen,
Whose Spirit Controlled the Various Groups of Life that Surrounded them
Through Power, from the Creator, did Not Try to Subdue each other.

They
Were Aware
Of each other
But Remained Apart.

The Amens
Tended to Roam within the warmer center of the land of Earth
And the Souls Moved in their Creatures
To the fringes of the Light of Day that Came from the Galaxy.

Now Light
Came only on one side of Earth,
That side with land
That sat within the Seas,[23]

Now as Time Passed, and Vegetation Grew in Abundance,
Fierce and huge Beasts
That Rivaled the Dinosaurs
Thrived in all parts of the land.

And they began to Overwhelm and Kill those bodies Entered by Souls.
And even the Amens could Not Control
The most savage and largest of Beasts,
Some that had Mixed with Reptiles Hatched in Bael's Caves.

Now Amens,
Who Communicated Among themselves by Thought and Motion,
Desired to Protect themselves from the Onslaught of Beasts.
The Wants and Needs of the Amen were simple.

Their Knowledge and Emotions
Were Directed toward their Relationship with the Almighty
and Survival on Earth.
But they Turned their Minds to Existence.

From under the Earth
They Discovered Gases
That could be Contained
In the skins of Animals.

They Found they could Explode these skins
Filled with those gases
With a simple Crystal Beamed from a ray of Light
From the Galaxy.

They also soon Observed that certain gases
That Filled the larger Animal skins would Rise above the Earth.
And could be Devised to Carry them on the winds
That Moved ever outward from the center of their lands.

They found that
On the higher levels the winds Moved ever inward
As the Earth Rotated on the lands
That were ever toward the Light of the Galaxy.

Then the Amens Contacted the Souls that had Entered the Primates
And they Prepared to Combat the fierce and huge Beasts, together.
But a great Disaster Befell them—
And much of the Third Heaven.

Bael Discovers the Power of Light
Bael was Emerged in the Pure White Light
But he was Able to only Contemplate upon it.
But in his Thinking about Light
He Pondered the Creation of the mass from Light.

By his great intuitive Reasoning
He also Pondered about his own Transposition,
And other Heavenly Spirits,
From Spirit to a Coagulated Form.

By Use of the force he had Converted himself from Spirit to Substance.
He Deduced
That this might be the Key to the Structuring of the I AM
And the Renewal.

Bael Deduced
That if he could Control Light,
God would Know that he, Bael,
Could Manage the Renewal.

God, who had Absorbed the total Knowledge of that which WAS,
Had Produced All in the I AM from this Enlightenment,
Through the Mind of God and the Eye of God, with the force
And His Own Growth of Self.

He had Made Each Creation in a Sequential Pattern—
Or with Thought that was Parallel,
If, that which was New,
Was something of a different nature.

Thus the Heavens were Complex but Logically Systematic and in Harmony,
With the Use of the force,
Designed by the Mind of God and the Eye of God,
In their Building and Maintenance.

The force was Utilized
In the I AM
Parallel to the Composition of God, the Trinity
And the I AM.

The major part of the force
Had from the Beginning of the I AM
Created and Sustained the Vastness of the I AM, all its Heavens
And its Surge with Light Against the Void.

But there was a portion of the force that Deviated,
Similar to the Trinity,
And Maintained Vast amounts of Related things, bodies and masses
In Unrelated Order to the Whole.

But These were Brought into Harmony
With All in the I AM.
But All was ever Changing with Newness
And No thing was Static.

The Bringing Forth of Spirits, Life and Kingdom of the Lord,
Through the special Vision of the Mind of God and Eye of God,
Had Caused a Syllogistic and Orderly Deviation
Of the Primacy of Material Creation by God in the Heavens.

The Creator
Through the Mind of God and Eye of God,
Had become Focused on the Living Earthly Beings
And the Kingdom of the Seventh Heaven.

Thus, when Bael began to Deliberate
Upon the Formation, Composition and nature of Light
To the Whole of the I AM,
The Almighty was Involved otherwise than on the Materiality of Light.

This Led God,
Though Aware,
Not to be fully Cognizant
Of the Extreme Thoughts of Bael.

When the Accomplished Archangel Theorized on the Makeup of Light,
He Conjectured that its Transference into mass
Was of the same Orderly and Parallel Process
That Allowed Spirit to become Dense.

Bael Surmised that the Ability to Control Light,
With the force,
Was Simple
And by its Use he could Find the Solution or Regulating the I AM.

Thus he could Prove his Competence
With this Deciphering of Light
And God would Consider him Over the Amilous
In the Ruling of the Renewal.

It was then Bael Chose the Third Heaven
For the Display of his Knowledge of Light—
Not only to Impress God,
But also Michael, who was in Charge of the Third Heaven.

Bael Chose Not just a small Light Source but a Galaxy.
When Bael, with his Limited Use of the force,
Reversed the Light of the Galaxy,
He was Not Expecting that which Happened.

The Entire Structure of Light,
That was Reversed by the Use of the force,
Was of such Intensity
That it Passed Through its Coagulation of mass.[24]

The Powers of the Inversion
Disrupted the Harmony
Of the Entire Third Heaven,
Including the Earth.

Because the Almighty Spirit
Through the Mind of God and the Eye of God,
Was Aware of All,
Even though Not Concentrating on them,

He Righted the Third Heaven,
Through the Mind of God and the Eye of God
With his Great Knowledge of the force,
Into a Harmony.

But All was Not as before.
For there was Darkness and Derangement
Upon the Deep of the Third Heaven Surround
Caused by the Light Inversion.

And the Earth was Convulsed and Thrust Into Blackness.
The Earth was without Form of Life
And Void of Life Upon its surface—except for those Suspended
In the Crystals of Ice that Formed after a Scorching Heat.

And God,
As soon as Harmony was in the Third Heaven,
Cast Bael
Into the Void.

Light Is Returned, with Life and Man Envisioned
Immense Disruption was in that Area of the Third Heaven
That Surrounded the Reversal of light
Caused by Bael.
Blackness was in that Expanse.

And the Earth, without the Energy of Light,
Was on its surface Absent of the Movement of Life
For it was Covered with the Crystals of Ice[25]
From the Cold of the Darkness.

Then the Creator Made it Known,
"The Heavens and Earth shall be Restored.
And the Earth and the Heavens
Shall be Filled with that which I Desire.

I shall Form
All that is Good,
And Alter those I wish Changed.
I shall Form a new Being.

Though the Being shall Be of Flesh and Blood as are the Amen,
It shall Be in the Image of the Lord God and the First Angels
And the Souls shall be Able to Enter the New Being
Instead of the varied Beasts.

And with the Amen,
He Shall have Dominion Over the Earth.
I shall Call the New Being,
Man.

And on the Earth
It shall be Known as the time of Man.
And when a Soul Enters Man,
It shall Remember Not as it Being Before."

Thus it was,
At the Commencement
Of the Time
Of Man.

Then the Great Spirit, El,
With the Mind of God and the Eye of God, and the force,
Concentrated Upon the Earth and its Surrounding Heavens
To Make New the Devastation Caused by Bael.

Genesis[26]
Beginning,
God Made True Shape of the Earth and its Heavens.
For the Earth was without its Form and its surface was Void
And Darkness was on the Deep that Encompassed it.

Then the Great Spirit, El,
Through the Mind of God and the Eye of God, with the force,
Moved all things in the Deep
As if by a Mighty Wind.

God Designed,
"Let there be Light."
And Light masses were Formed.
And God Saw it was Good.

And the Light was Separated from the Darkness,
For the Almighty Left Vast Areas without masses of Light
In the Third Heaven
To Remember the Chaos Caused by Bael.

Now the Earth in the Third Heaven
Was at the Edge of the masses of Light that had been Formed.
And the Earth was Revolved
To Absorb the Light.

And the Earth,
From the Warming of the Light and the Winds,
Was Covered with Water
From the Crystals of Ice.

The Creator had always Called
The Particles of Light Coming Upon the Earth,
From the Galaxy, Day.
And the Earth's Dark side that Followed, Night.

The Glow of Light Approaching the Edge of Earth He Called Morning
And the Opposite side Dimness was Named Evening.
Now the Revolvement of the Earth was Made Different and
There was a Continuous Changing of Light and Darkness upon its surface.

And as always, Parallel to before,
God Called where the Light Fell on Earth, day,
And the Darkness, night.
And there was day and night on the face of the Earth.

And on the first day as it changed,
There was an evening and a morning on the Earth.
Then God Created the Shield of water and elements
Above the waters of the face of the Earth to Moderate the Energy and Heat

Of the Light of day and the Darkness of the night.
And the Shield was Called the heaven of Earth.
And there was a second evening and morning
Upon the second day of Earth.

Then God Commanded that Ocean waters
Be Gathered on one side of Earth
And the lands of Earth Appear and Be Separated into three,
By waters Called Seas.

And a Seepage of waters Be Beneath the soil.
And it was So.
And God Saw
It was Good.

And from the melted Crystals of Ice,
God Called Forth
The vegetation of the Earth
That He Desired—

From the smallest of plants to the largest,
And the grasses, the herbs, the fruits,
And all those that would be of their own kind
And their own seed.

And it was So.
And God was Pleased.
And a day
Passed Upon the Earth.

Now the Earth was Separate and Apart
At the edge of the Light
That Railed Against the Dark Confusion
Caused by Bael.

And God Commanded that,
"One Light shall be Set to Warm the Earth
And Cause the Life to Grow.
And it shall Cause the day and night Upon the Earth.

And it shall Cause a lesser Light to Rule the night
And bring Seepage to the Soil.
And it will Be such that there will be
Seasons Upon the Earth[27]

And Let the Stars Be Set
And Planets—
To Be Signs to Man."
And it was So.

And, by the Sun and Moon, Ended the Fourth Day
Then God Conveyed, "Bring Forth the Moving Creatures
And those that Fly, that they may have Life
From their Suspension in the waters that were Frozen."

Then God Created
All manner of Whale
To Dominate those from before in the Oceans.
And the Fifth day Passed.

Then from the elements,
God Created those Creatures He Desired.
Creatures that would Sustain Man,
All those Creatures that Kept Close to the Earth.

And each was of their own kind,
With Coils of Life to Multiply.
And God Placed Amen on their own lush land
And God Saw it was Good and the Earth was Ready.

And God Conveyed to the Lord God and the Amilous,
"Let us Make Man in our Own Image, after our Likeness of Angels.
And God Created Man in His Own Likeness.
In flesh and blood He Made them, though each was different.

Equally,
Male and female,
Twelve times twelve thousand He Created them,[28]
To Be on their own land.

And each was Entered with a Soul by their Desire
And the Desire of the Amilous.
And each was with Coils of Life
And each was different, though of kind.

Then God Conveyed, "Be Blessed and Multiply.
I have Given you Dominion over all the Earth that I have Made.
All that which is New is yours to eat."
And God Beheld All that He had Created and it was Good.

And it was the End of the Sixth day on the land of Man.
Then the Creator Blessed the Earth and its heavens
At the Beginning of the Seventh day and Sanctified it.
And the Almighty Rested His Concentration.

Effects of Bael
While the Almighty, El, Renewed the Third Heaven and the Earth,
Bael, Exiled into the Eternal Darkness,
Absorbed the Cast Out Negative Emotions.
And Bael became Morose at his Rejection By God.

Now Bael Knew
That God Loved all Life
Then on the Renewed Earth,
For He had Called it Good.

And Bael Knew that some of the Life on Earth
That had been Formed before the Turmoil,
Was Not Re-formed by God,
But had Not Died.

That Life
Was Suspended in Remote Crystals of Ice.
For Bael had Ruled the Earth
And was Aware.

Then, Bael, who was Banished to the Void,
Called Upon Belzebel and Michael
To Revive all the Life they Possibly Could
That was on Earth Prior to his Reversal of Light.

And the Two,
Who had been Comrades of Bael, Did.
And some of the Reptiles and Insects of Bael
Were Brought Forth from eggs in the Caves of Bael.

Though much old Life did Not Resuscitate.
And some Life which was Good and Newly Formed by God,
Mixed with that, which had Formed itself by the Coils of Life
And the Corruptions of Bael.

And God was Irate at Michael and Belzebel.
Now, God, though Angered,
Felt great Love for Michael,
And Sent him to the Purification of the First Heaven.

But Belzebel,
For a Degree of Time,
Was Cast into the Outer Darkness with Bael.
The Almighty Reflected Upon all which had Transpired.

For with the Disturbance by Bael,
The Harmony of Universes in the Third Heaven of the I AM
Had Changed
With other than the Mind of God and the Eye of God.

It was the First such Occurrence.
In All the Time of the I AM.
And the Almighty, El,
Pondered Upon the Event and its Results.

Man and Amen

Now the nature of Man and Amen was different.
Amen's Spirit nature was Directly from God
And Merged into their Beastly flesh and blood.
Amen Controlled their flesh and blood with their Spirit from God.

And, Except for Finding Sustenance for their bodies
And Seeing to the Well-being of others,
Amen Only Worshiped God
And all that He Made.

When Souls Entered the flesh and blood of the Offspring of Man
As they had when they Entered the Beasts—
Their Emotions Changed
To Coincide with the Needs and Desires of Life.

Souls
Were only Peripherally Aware
Of their Spirit nature while in Man,
But they Perceived that they were Not as the Beasts.

Much was the Confusion of Man
And great was their Perplexity in the Arrangements of all on Earth.
They Knew from the Pronouncement of God that
They were to Dominate the Earth, but they Remembered Not their God.

Far different than Amen,
Soul's Spirit
Was Not Attached
To the nature of God.

Souls were from the Amilous and the Angels.
They were Free-willed Spirits in flesh and blood
With only a slight Impression within them of their Past.
Thus Man could Not Comprehend their Being.

Angels Are Sent to Earth to Guide and Rule Man
Then God Sent Angels to Rule and Guide the new Formed Man.
And these Angels were Given the Title of King.
And the Amilous who Watched Over them
Was Called the King of Kings.

Now the Amilous Knew the weakness
Of the elemental Structure of the Earthly Forms of Angels.
And through God, Caused them to be Sustained on Earth
With the Breathing of a Variety of special Aromas,

The Creation of the Needed elements in the Trees of Life to eat,
The Absorption of the Sun and Gold on their Radiant skins
And water Purified of Salt.
Angels were Forbidden great amounts of Salt.

For an Excess of Salt
Disintegrated their Formed essence
And Returned them
To their Spirit nature.

The Angels Lived in High Places of Earth,
To be Free of the Salt Filled waters and to Feel the Sun rays, and to
Enjoy the fragrances that Filtered to them
And Raise the Trees of Life.

And Man Lived in the lands Below them.
Man, male and female, Maintained themselves as best they could.
And they Visited the Magnificent stone Structures
Built by the Angel Kings,

Who Used their great Knowledge
In the Cutting and Movement of the great rocks.
And Man and Amen Aided their Angel Kings
In the Formation of their Kingdoms.

In Exchange for Knowledge, Instruction and Worship, Man and Amen
    Gave
Gifts, Aromatic Scents and Sacrifices of the First and Finest
Of their food Gatherings and Catches for Burning—
Which was for the Angels the most Pleasing of all the fragrances.

And God and the Trinity were Pleased
With the Earth, the Development of Man and their Souls
And their Advancement in Control of the Earth
By the Guidance of Angels.

Now, as the nature of All,
No two things or Beings were Alike,
Though each Kind's Form
Was Similar.

But as each group of Man, male and female, began to Develop
Under the Guidance of Each King.
They Began to Appear with different Features
So that each Angel King Knew his people.

Then as Time Passed
Those on the center land division of the King Atlel
Developed in Knowledge
More than all the rest.

And with large polished Pyramid Crystals
The Angel Kings Used the Rays of the Sun
To Develop great Comforts for them
And those Chosen Souls within Man.

But the Amen
Desired Not
These Types of Ease and Pleasures
And they Kept to themselves.

Return of Michael and Belzebel
Ending their Measurement of Time,
Michael and Belzebel Returned to the Heavens.
But Bael was Left in the Darkness.
Thus, Michael was Repentant and he was in Spirit in the Heavens.

But Belzebel was Returned to Earth
To Live In Earthly Form
As Half Archangel
And Half Amphibian in the Oceans.

Again the Great Spirit Let it Be Known
That He was Infinite in His Satisfaction
At the Atonement of Michael,
A Capricious son of God.

And all of the Heavenly Beings, especially the Souls,
Were Jubilant at the Favorable Return of Michael.
But when Belzebel Returned to Rule his Ocean and Seas,
God Made No Pronouncement of Pleasure.

For the Almighty Knew
That Belzebel
Was in Constant Contact with Bael
In the Abyss.

For Belzebel was Not Sure
Whether Bael of the Amilous would Rule the Renewal
And the Vacillating Belzebel
Wished to Be on the Triumphant one's side.

Bael Turns from God and Creates Havoc In All the I AM
Now in the Abyss,
Bael Consumed Extreme Amounts of Negative Emotions.
And his nature Reversed.
And Bael Completely Turned From the Love of God.

But the Last Formed Archangel Grew in Amazing Dimensions
Of Negative Emotions, Knowledge, Power, Thrust and Energy.
Now even the Great Spirit was Not Aware of All in the Void—
Especially that which had Happened to Bael.

And Bael, who had Controlled the Fiery First Heaven
Knew it was the First Heaven that was the Beginning Creation of the I AM.
Bael had also Reversed Light
With his Known Power of the force.

Now Bael Controlled the Vast Void
And his Desire for Power was now Unlimited.
Then Bael Suddenly Pulled Power From the force
Into the Abyss.

For the force does Not Distinguish its Power for any Specific Use.
The Almighty of the I AM Always had Controlled the Balance of the force.
But when the Counter Surge was Thrust
Upon the I AM,

The Harmony of the Mind of God and Eye of God
Was Briefly Counteracted.
A Turmoil was Found
In All of the I AM

And Enormous Flashes of Light Pierced All the Heavens
From the Disruption of the Harmony—
Even in the Pure Light
Of the First Heaven.

Only the Second Heaven
Shielded the other Heavens
From Disaster,
By its Pull.

Then Bael, through his Use of the force, Conveyed to All,
"For the I AM, it is Time for its End.
Now I Bael,
Will be the New Ruler of the World.

All Heavenly Beings
Are to Come Unto Me.
The Abyss is the Renewal of the World
Into the NEXT TIME."

And with the Dissonance of the I AM, Bael, with the force,
Caused the Light that Moved Against the Dark Void,
To Oppose itself and Form an enormous Blaze of Light
At the Border of the I AM and the Abyss.

Then Bael Conveyed, "I am the New Light. Come Unto me."
Then a Multitude of Angels Led by Sammael, Head of the Seraphim;
Ariel, Chief of the Potentates;
Camael, Chief of the Powers;

And all of the Souls—
Except those in the Remnants of Man
That Survived the Turmoil that Effected the Heavens and Earth
Who Followed Belzebel; these Crossed Over Into the Abyss with Bael.[29]

Then Bael Made Known, "Belzebel is the Prince of Darkness
And will Sit At my Right Hand.
Sammael is Head of all the Angels in the Abyss
And shall Sit At my Left Hand,

Camael is Chief of all Angels of Darkness that Shall Rule
That which was the I AM and Sit Before me.
Ariel is Chief of the Souls
And shall Sit Down and Behind me."

Now the Surge,
With the Limited Powers of the force Exploited by Bael,
Did Not Prevail
Against the Mind of God and Eye of God.

And the Almighty of the I AM
With the Use of the Tremendous Power with the force,
Counteracted the Actions of Bael
Toward the Harmony of the Heavens.

But the great Confusion of Angels and Souls were still in the Void,
Though most Angels had Not Crossed Over.
And only three, of the Eleven Heads and Chiefs of Angels,
Were in the Abyss with Bael and Belzebel, the Archangels.

Now,
The Spirit of God,
Or the Light of the I AM,
Does Not Enter the Void.

Light, with the Use of the force,
Through the Mind of God and Eye of God,
Subdues the Edges of the Chaos of Darkness
Forming All New things of the I AM.

Thus
The Angels and the Souls in the Void
Could Not Be Returned to the I AM
By God.

Now Michael, though often Errant,
Loved God with Emotions just Below those of the Trinity.
And Michael Instantly became Tuned In Entirely with God
Through this Love.

And God Knowing,
Gave Michael
Great Power of the force
To Use Against that of Bael.

Now nearly one third of all the Angels
And most all of the Souls
Had Transported themselves into the Abyss
For they Thought the Settling of the World had been Given to Bael.

And Bael had Immediately Transmuted Emotions of Evil,
That had been Thrust into the great Chaos,
Into those Beings
Who had Come Into the Darkness.

And,
With his Limited Use of the force,
Bael Cast Back Into the I AM
Much of the Beings' Positive Emotions.

And Bael
Ruled the Darkness of the Void
With all those Beings
Who had Come to him.

The Amilous, Michael and The Metatron Save Many Angels and the Souls

Now once again
The I AM was in Harmony
And the Omnipotent God
Controlled the Heavens.

Then the Amilous, Michael and The Metatron
Swept into the Void.
And All those in the Heavens were Stunned,
For they Thought that the Trio had Gone Over to Bael.

But the Amilous, Michael and The Metatron, Using their Endowment
Of the force by God, which together far Exceeded that Power of Bael,
Brought Back nearly all of the Souls
And those Angels Not Hopelessly Inverted with their Emotions.

Before the Threesome,
Could Escape the Abyss,
Bael Enveloped them
With Negative Emotions.

But the nature of the Amilous,
Refined with the Pure Light of the First Heaven,
Repelled the Negative Emotions
Of the Chaos.

And Bael,
In the Recesses of his Mind,
Recalled his Love for Michael
And this Left Michael Free of the Evil in the Darkness.

But The Metatron
Felt the Dreaded Sin—
Vanity—
Permeate within his Spirit.

Then the Almighty Secured the Heavens,
With the force.
And the Points of Light
Overcame the Rim of Darkness of Bael.

And God Proclaimed, "No longer shall the Last Formed Archangel
Be Known as Bael,
But shall be Called Baal, the Satan, the Adversary.
He sail be Known as the King of Darkness.

Since he Desires to Rule,
He shall Rule the Chaos of the Abyss
Until Light
Triumphs Over All the Darkness.

Then Baal, the Satan,
Shall Be Stripped of all his Powers—
Or should he Repent he will once again Be Welcomed
Into the Light and the Ways of God of the I AM that I AM.

All, who are now in the Void or Enter it,
Will Suffer Torment to their Emotions
Until All is Brought Together—
Which is Infinity.

Returned Angels
Corrupted by Baal, the Satan, During their Time in the Abyss,
Shall Dwell Upon the Earth in their Corporeal Forms
So their Spirits do Not Disrupt the Heavens.

They shall be in the land of Atla,[30]
And the Lord God,
Within the Trinity, and with Angels of the Lord,
Shall Guide them Until they are Pure."

Then the Great Spirit, El
Who Desired to Concentrate Upon the Restoration
And Protection
Of the Seven Heavens,

Gave the Trinity
The Use of the Mind of God and the Eye of God,
With the force,
The Rite of Regeneration of the Angels and Souls.

And the Lord God was Endowed with the Power,
Through the Mind of God and the Eye of God,
With the force,
To Refurbish the Earth and all upon it.

Then the Amilous,
Whose Sacrifice with the Angels,
Had Fostered the Making of the Souls,
Was Desirous of Redeeming the Souls from the Evils of the Abyss.

And the Amilous
Wished to Sacrifice More of Himself
To Rid the Souls of their Taint of Evil
Acquired in the Abyss.

But God
Did Not Wish to Take Away any More from the Power of the Amilous,
For He Knew Not what Bael was Going to Do
In the Future.

Now those Amens already Merged with God,
Knowing these Thoughts of God,
Desired to Sacrifice of their Spirit
For the Redemption of the Souls.

They would Give Part of their Spirits
To Enter Men and Women so to Aid their Souls.
The Spirit of Amen would Help to Guide the Souls to the Love of God
From the Evils of those Given by Baal to them in the Darkness.

And the Great Spirit, El, Agreed.
Then the Almighty Conveyed, "The Sacrificial Spirits of the Amen
Shall Pass as Needed into Men and Women,
Directed by the Amilous and the Holy Spirit.

The Spirits of the Amen
Shall Guide the Souls within Man
To Be Purified of the Evil of the Abyss.
And the name of Amen shall Be On the Lips of Man Forever.

Now Souls shall No Longer be Separate
From the flesh and blood of Man.
The essence of the Soul's Spirit
Shall Enter and be fully Attached within Man.

Man shall Be a Living Soul of flesh and blood
And his Breath shall Know the Spirit of Amen from God to Guide him.
And as in Amen, part of the Pure Spirit of Amen
Shall Pass On to the Children of Man.

The Spirit of Souls,
The Pure Amen Spirit from God and the flesh and blood
Shall Be as One until the flesh Dies.
Then the Spirits of Man shall Return to their Spirit nature.

And the Spirit of Amen
That is Not Passed On to the Sons and Daughters of Man
Shall Return to God.
And the Spirit of Souls which are Purified shall Pass Into the Heavens.

Those Souls that Need Further Redemption
Shall be Bound to the Torments that were Devised by Baal
In the First Heaven or If Not Redeemable
Shall be Cast Into the Darkness Forever Until the End of TIME."

Thus the Earth
Became the Focal Point of the great Conflicts
For the Redemption of the Tainted Spirits of Angels and Souls.
And Baal, the Satan, Knew.

The Lord God Regenerates the Earth and Its Heaven
The same Harmony of the masses No Longer Surrounded the Earth
As before the Turmoil of Baal.
The Sun, the Moon and the Planet Masses were Not as they had been
In their Rotation and Order.

And there was a different Alignment
Of the masses
Of Light
And the Universes.

But with the Knowledge of the Mind of God and Eye of God
And with the Power of the force,
The Lord God Realigned the Heavens about the Earth.
Then the Lord God Caused the Dome of Earth's heaven to be Fully
    Formed.

Then the Angels,
That had Absorbed the Evils of the Abyss from Baal,
Were Placed in their Corporeal Forms
Upon the islands of Atla.

And Atla was Filled
With Herbs for their Aroma,
The Trees of Life
And the lands were Filled with Gold to Sustain the Angels.

And high were the Mountains on the center land of Atla
And fresh were the waters that Rose from beneath the Atla lands.
And the Angels of God Also Came Upon the Atla lands
To Guide the Angels of Baal to their Redemption with God.

And those Amens and Man that Survived the great Turmoil
Were Scattered
On all the lands of Earth
But Atla.

And their nature was still that as before.
And the Remnant of original Man
Was Not Entered with Spirit from the Merged Amen of God
But those of Man that Lived were Entered by Souls Not Attached.

The Formation of the Man Adam and the Woman Eve[31]
These then were the Generations of the Heavens and Earth
And as they were Created,
And in the day that the Lord God Completed
The Earth and its heaven.

Now No Vegetation or Herb was on the lands.
And in those days there was Not rain
Bur water Rose from Under the earth
To Cause all to Grow.

And the Lord God Formed a Man of the elements of the land
And Breathed Into him the Amen Spirit
And by the Soul's Entry and Joining with the flesh and blood
A Man Became a Living Soul.

Then for the Man,
The Lord God Made a Garden Eastward in the land of Eden.
And Caused to Grow every Tree that was Pleasant
And all foods that were Good.

And He Entered a Tree of Life
For the Angels of God that Accompanied Him.
And He Formed a Tree
That He Called the Tree of Knowledge,

For He Planned to Enter it with all of the Evil
That was Released from the Man by the Spirit.
For the Lord God Did Not Wish this Evil
To Pass Over into the Abyss with Baal.

For He Knew Not
The Actions
Of Baal
Toward it.

The land of the Man
Was Filled with Gold and Precious Stone and Wondrous Rivers.
And the Man was Placed in this Garden of Eden
To Attend it.

Then the Lord God Spoke to the Man.
For this was the First Time
There was a Spoken Word to Man
And that Man Could Speak.

And God Commanded with His First Words,
"You May Eat of every Tree but that of the Knowledge of Good and Evil
For in the day that you Eat of it
You will Surely Die the Death of Darkness."

And the Man Understood.
And it has been Recorded
Since then
By Spokesman Heirs.

Baal, Using the Powers of the force,
Made himself Aware of all the Emotions and Knowledge
Of those Angels and Souls
That had Returned to the Heavens from the Chaos.

And Being Baal,
He was Also Aware
Of what the Lord God had Done
With the Tree of Knowledge.

Adam
Then the Lord God Called the Man
Of Spirit, Soul and blood within his flesh, Adam.[32]
For Adam was Made
Of the Elements of the Soil.

Then the Lord God Spoke,
"I shall Bring Into Paradise
Those Creatures I Desire
And there will be those for Companions of Adam."

And from the elements
The Lord God Formed those Creatures He Desired.
He Brought the Beasts to Adam
To Find what he would Call them.

And whatever Name
That Adam Spoke,
That was the Name
They were Called.

But None of the Beasts
Were a Mate for Adam—
Though One was such that Adam Desired,
For Lust was in the Soul of Adam.

But as Time Passed the Evil
That had Come Into the Soul of Adam in the Abyss,
Was Cast Out by the Guiding Spirit
Into the Tree of Knowledge.

Then Adam Became the Perfection of Man
As Desired by the Lord God.
And Adam was to Be the Model of all those of Man
Whose Soul would Be Redeemed by the Spirit within him—of Amen.

Then the Lord God Said, "I will now Make a Help Mate for Adam."
Then the Lord God
Placed Adam into a Sleep
And Took a Part From him.

Then from the Ribbon of Life of Adam—
From Adam's flesh and blood—
The Lord God with the elements of the Earth
Made a woman.

And she was as the Perfection of Adam
And they were as One
For she was From him—
Yet they were Separate.

And the Lord God Perceived
That the Heirs of Adam and the Woman
Would Fulfill the Atonement
Of all the Souls from the Evil of the Darkness.

And the Lord God was Pleased.
And Adam Knew.
Then Adam said, "This Woman's bone is From my bone
And her flesh is from my flesh and we are as One."

And our Purity shall enter Men and Women.
And the Children of Man
Shall Leave their Fathers and Mothers and Cleave Unto Each Other.
And they shall Be as One flesh as are we."

And
They Knew Love
For Each Other
In their Nakedness.

Baal Deceives the Lord God
Now, Baal,
Who still was able to control the Thoughts of Reptiles on the Earth,
Entered a Serpent Into
The Paradise of Adam.

Now, with Baal, the Serpent was More Cunning and Devious
Than any of the Beasts that the Lord God had Made.
Then Baal, with the force,
Shielded Eden from the Lord God.

Then, through the Serpent,
Baal Enticed the Woman of Adam to Eat of the Tree of Knowledge
That the Lord God had Cast the Evils, from Adam and the Woman
Into.

For the Serpent had Told her
She would Know Good and Evil and Be as a God.
And the Woman
Gave of the Fruit of the Tree to Adam.

And their Souls
Were Again Filled
With the Knowledge and Emotions of Evil
That had been Absorbed in the Darkness.

And they were Naked
And their Lust Overpowered their Love.
Then Adam and his Mate
Fell into a deep Sleep.

Now the Lord God
Had Prepared to Take From Adam
His Perfection
Through his Coils of Life,

Then Mix With a Coil of Life
Within the five most Fair of females
In the five Kingdoms
Of the Remnants of Original Man.

Their Offspring
Would be Entered by a Living Soul
And the Spirit from the Purified Adam.
Their Kingdom's Unique Features would be Retained.

And Baal Knew.
When the Lord God
Came Into the Garden
Baal Withdrew
The Mantle of force from Adam.

And the Lord God
Took the Coils of Life from the Sleeping Adam
And Entered them into the five females
In their Kingdoms.

Then the Lord God Came Into Eden to Tell Adam.
But Baal Hid Adam and the Woman from the Lord.
But the Lord Pursued in Finding them.
Then Baal Lifted the force from Eden and Returned thoughts to the
    Abyss.

And the Lord God Found of Baal's Deception
And the Corruption of Adam and Eve.
Then He Cursed the Serpent to Crawl in the Dust
Forever;

And Foretold
That Because of the Knowledge of Evil,
The Head of the Children of Adam would Enlarge
And Multiply the Pains of Women in Childbirth;

And the Heirs of Adam
Would Work Forever to Acquire their food.
And Adam Remembered
And Recorded the Curse of the Lord to his Heirs.

Then the Lord God,
Not Aware of Baal's Motives from the Abyss Declared,
"Only the Wife of Adam
Will have Offspring who will be Entered by the Living Soul.

Thus though the Spirit
Was Passed On to the Children of the five females in the Five Kingdoms
Through the Coils of Life of Adam,
The Souls Entering their five Offspring were Not Attached.

And
The Amen Spirit
Was of No Avail
To their Free-willed Souls.

Now Adam Had Named his Wife, Eve,
For she would be the Only Mother of Living Souls.
But Adams Offsprings' Perfect Stature and Spirit of Amen
Enhanced the Five Kingdoms of Original Man.

Then Adam and Eve were Cast Out of Eden, As Recorded.
Then Cain was Born from the Lust of Adam and Eve.
And the Lord God Knew the Evil in his Soul.
Eve Again Conceived a son, Abel. And the Lord God Blessed his Soul.

Now Cain Harvested Grains from the Earth
And Abel Tended Beasts Known as Cattle.
And Each Offered, of their First and Finest,
A Burnt Offering to the Lord God.

And as the Angels,
The Lord God Enjoyed the Fragrance of Burnt Offerings.
But Most of all He Liked the Odor
Of the Burnt Offerings of the flesh and fats of Cattle.

And there was Jealousy in the Soul of Cain,
For the Lord God Favored the Sacrifices of Abel
More than those of grain of Cain.
And the Lord God Knew.

And the Lord God said to Cain, "Why are you Angered?
For I will Reward you,
As I do Abel,
If you do Well."

But Even the Lord God
Did Not Understand
The Manner that Evil from the Abyss
Would Arise in the nature of the Soul within the flesh of Man.

For the Manner of Emotions of the Embedded and Tainted Soul
Within the flesh was Different from anything Before.
Then the Lord God said to Cain, "You are the Oldest
And you will Rule Over Abel if you do Well."

But Cain was Morose.
And he Called to his Brother Abel to Come into his field.
And when Abel Came,
Cain Rose Up and Slew him.

Now,
Until that Time,
Neither Amen or Man
Had Ever Killed one another Deliberately.

Now the Lord God was Aware of the Evil within Cain
And when He Smelled the Odor of the Blood,
He Asked of Cain where was his Brother.
And Cain Replied, "Am I my Brother's Keeper."

Then the Lord God Knew what had been Done.
And He Cast Cain Out even the edges of Eden
And Cursed him.
But when Cain Repented, the Lord God Reduced his Punishment.

And Cain Went Into the land with the Remnants of Original Man
On the land of Nod.
And he Took to himself a Wife
Who Bore him children.

And Cain was the First of Man to Build a City,
Which he Named after his First Son Enoch.
And Cain and all his Children and Children's Children
Brought the Spirit to Man and the Living Soul within Man.

And Adam and Eve had another Son, Called Seth.
And Seth was Blessed by God.
And all of Seth's Children and Children's Children
Brought the Spirit to Man and the Soul Attached Within Man.

And great were the Offspring of Adam and Eve Among Man.
But all would Be Entered
With the Souls Filled with the Evils of the Abyss,
Because of the Folly of Adam and Eve.

The Spirit of The Metatron Enters Man
Now Man had only been Entered by the Souls.
But The Metatron, who was Filled with Vanity
From the time he had Entered the Darkness to Save the Angels and
    Souls,
Asked God to Rid him of this Evil.

And God said,
"You may Enter the Body of a Man
And with the Spirit of the Perfect Amen,
You may Rid your Imperfection."

And the Spirit of The Metatron was Entered into the Lineage of Seth,
As the Offspring of Jared
And he Inherited the Amen Spirit
And he also was Called Enoch.

Now never before had an Angel Entered Into Man.
And Enoch was a giant in Stature and Knowledge among Man.
Enoch Recorded, by his Son, Methuselah, as Spokesman to all their
    Heirs,
The Sins of Adam and Eve.

Then Enoch
Walked with God Upon the Earth
And was Taken again into Heaven.[33]
For he was of Perfection.

The Angels Take to Wife the Daughters Man[34]
Now the Angels Residing Upon Atla Began to Move About the Earth
From land to land by Craft of Air and Sea,
Some Powered by the Crystals of Light
Atop the great Pyramid on the Mountain of Atlas.

Now the Angels
Found the Daughters of Man
To be of Beauty,
Especially those Heirs of Adam and Eve.

Now the Angels in the Corporeal Forms
Were Not as flesh and blood
And they were Neither Male or Female, but Both,
But they Could Not Bear Offspring.

But the Angels of Baal Found that through the Daughters of Man,
Children could Be Born from them.
And their Offspring were Great among Man
In Stature and Knowledge.

Now the Children of the Angels of Baal
Were Called Nephilim,
As were those of the Angels of God,
Offspring of Nephilim were Raphiem.

Then the Angels of Baal Took to Wife
As many of the Daughters of Man as they Pleased.
But the Angels of God
Took Only One.

Belzebel Returns to Earth
Now Belzebel Requested of God
To Return to the Heavens from the Darkness.
But God Knew Not Why Belzebel Decided to Return.
For He did Not Know those Events that Went On in the Abyss of Baal.

Then God Allowed Belzebel
To Return to his Oceans Upon the Earth
But Nowhere else could he Be
In the Heavens.
　　　　　　　　·

And then God said, "You shall be Known as Belzebub,
For you are Tainted from the Abyss
And No One in the Heavens or Earth
Is to Know you as an Archangel of God."

And Belzebub
Came Into the Ocean
With half the body of an Archangel
And half Amphibian.

The Corruption of the Beings on Earth
Now the Angels
At their Creation Upon the Earth
Had the nature of both male and female
Within their Bodies.

But the Angels could Bear No Children.
The Nephilim,
The Offspring of the Angels by the daughters of Man,
Were all male in nature.

Nephilim too could have children by the females of Man.
And they were giants to Man.
Their Structure was the Combination of flesh and blood
And the Composition, Strength and Inherited Knowledge from Angels.

They were Entered by Souls,
But they were Not Able to Inherit the Spirit of the Amen of God
Through any female Heir
Of Adam and Eve.

But the Raphiem,
The Children of the Nephilim and the daughter of Man,
Were
Separated Into male and female.

But they also were great in Stature and Knowledge among Man.
And they too were Entered by Souls,
Though Never
The Spirit of the Amen of God.

But the Heirs of the Raphiem
Became more and more of the flesh and blood
If they were Born of the females of Man.
But to Man they were still Mighty and Known with Renown.

And the second generation
Could be Entered
By the Spirit of the Mother
If she were an Heir of Adam and Eve.

Now with the great Entry of the Evil of the Souls Into Man;
The Enhancement of this Evil
From the Many Tainted Angels of Baal or their Offspring
The Corrupted sons and daughters of the Angels of Baal—

Those Nephilim, Raphiem and Man,
Who were without Spirit to Guide them,
These Beings
Caused a great Depravity Upon the Earth.

The Angels of Baal,
Who began to Control all the Spiritless Beings,
Began to Pit Man against Man, male and female,
Nephilim Against other Nephilim and Raphiem, Groups against
      Groups.

And finally they began to Create Raids, Skirmishes and Battles
That Led Into great Wars.
And there were all nature of Atrocities
That Began.

And the sons of the Angels and Angels of Baal
Began to Alter the Coils of Life in all flesh—
Even with Man.
And Souls began to Come into all flesh that was part Man.

And the Souls
Entered those already with Souls.
And the flesh on Earth
Became Corrupt.

And the Lord God
Regretted all flesh that was Created on the Earth.[35]
And He was Angered
At the Evil Influence of those He Called the sons of Baal.

And it Embarrassed the Lord God
In the way He had Made a Man on the Earth
And how He had Allowed the Offspring to the Daughters of Man by
     Baal—
And the sons of God, many of whose Heirs became Corrupted.

Then Almighty God Contemplated the Destruction of all the flesh
That had been Created by the sons of Baal.
Only Noah, the son of the son of the son of Enoch (The Metatron)
Was found among Man to be Holy.

Thus only Noah found Favor with God
Then Almighty God said, "I will Flood the Earth's Corruption,
But the top of Atla,
To Save the Angels of God.

And of those of Soul and Spirit,
Only Noah will be Saved,
With his family.
All others shall Perish."

Then through the Lord God, the Almighty Told Noah
To Build an Ark of a certain Dimension
And to Load his family,
The Pure Animals of the Lord and vegetation to Grow.

Then Noah Did
And he Readied his sons, Shem, Ham and Japeth,
With all their Wives to Go.
All this is Recorded, for Noah was a Spokesman.

Belzebub Warns Many of Disaster
Now Belzebub,
Who Lived in the Oceans as half Amphibian and half Archangel in
    Form,
Learned from Baal of the Wrath of God, with and through the Lord God,
Toward the Earth.

And Belzebub Warned the Angels of Baal
And many of Man on the lands of Earth.
But few Heeded Belzebub and Prepared, especially those of Man.
For Man Knew Not who the Amphibian Archangel was.

Many Angels of Baal Enlarged their Crafts
To Rise Above the Waters or Within.
But only the Man, Xisuturous, the great Shipbuilder,[36]
Constructed an Ark, as did Noah.

Only the Peak of the Mountain Atlas,
That Housed
The Converged Angels of God,
Was to be Saved and Corruption Destroyed.

The Deluge
Then with great Disruption of the Earth and Tilting it,
The Lord God Shattered with great Upheavals
And Sank Forever two of the three Islands of Angels,
Leaving only Atla and its Mountain

And the Oceans Rose and Inundated all the lands of Corruption.
And the Dome of the waters of heaven was Broken
And it Rained for the First time Upon the Earth's lower lands
Causing the great Ice Remaining from the Upset of Baal, to Melt.

Now all that Happened to Noah
Is Recorded.
For Noah, an Heir of The Metatron,
Was a Spokesman.

But Noah Deleted
All Reference to the Presence of Og Upon the Ark,
For it was Og
Who Later Duped him.

And Noah Knew Not all that Happened Upon the Earth,
For the Lord God
Did Not Tell him of the Circumvention of Belzebub
And his Warning of others.

Though as was Told,
Noah and his sons and wives were the only True Heirs of Adam
With Soul and Spirit,
Left on the Earth following the great Flood.

And, Recorded by Noah, when the Deluge Subsided,
He and his family, Thankful for their Safety,
Prepared their most Glorious Aromas for the Lord God
With their Burnt Offerings.

Then Almighty God
Made His Covenant with Noah,
Whose family Remained the only Heirs of Adam,
That He would Not Destroy all Living Souls Again.

And to all the Heirs of Adam
He Granted the Sight of Beauty of a wide Spectrum of Colors,
Where before
Man's Vision of Color was Limited.

Then in the heavens, the Lord God Caused
A great Rainbow Above the Receding Flood-waters
For all the family of Noah to See its Colors—
Symbol of this Covenant.

The Remnants of Earth
Now
Though Great was the Destruction Upon the Earth,
Much of Life in the Oceans
Remained.

And on the fringes of the Earth
Furthest from the Inundation of vast Islands and Angels, many of Man,
A few of Amen and much of the Vegetation and Beasts
Remained.

For even before the Deluge was over
The Lord God Regretted His Anger against Life on Earth.
And Except for that around Noah, He Made the waters to Assuage.
This Saved a few Nephilim and Raphiem.

Those Angels of Baal that Rose Above the Deluge
Were Brought Again to the Island of Atla
For they had Defied God
By their Wandering Upon other lands.

Only the Kings of Man were to be so Privileged,
All Angels of God Survived.
All others Returned in Spirit
To the Heavens or Void.

Og Dupes Noah
Now Og[37]
Who with his twin brother Sihon,
Was the giant Raphiem son of the wife of Ham,
The second son of Noah.

His Nephilim father, Ahjah,
Son of the Angel Shamhazel,
Had Seduced the wife of Ham
Before she was married.

Og, who had Learned of the Deluge from Ham
Had Convinced Noah to Take him on the Ark
To Tend the Animals,
For he was strong beyond any Man.

And Further,
Og, Pledged to be the Servant of Noah and his Heirs Forever.
But when the waters Receded
Og was Not happy with his Fate.

Now at the time of the Covenant of God with Noah,
The family of Noah was Charged
With the Multiplying of the Creatures and Vegetation
From the Ark.

And Noah and his family became Herdsmen and Growers
To Spread Life Upon the Earth.
And Noah began to Grow Vineyards to Eat
And to Drink the Wine thereof

But Noah Knew Not the Treachery of Og.
For Belzebub was Informed by Og of the Wine of Noah's Vineyards.
Then, with Knowledge from Baal,
The Fermentation was Changed Into a great Drug.

And Noah,
With his sons, Shem, Ham, Japeth and Ham's son Canaan—
Who unerringly Aided Og—
Drank of the Wine and Fell Into a Profound Sleep.

Then the giant Og Carried them into the Caves of Baal,
Where they were in a Stupor Not before Known to Man.
And Og took their Wives and families,
And they Followed Og as He was the son of Ham's Wife.

And he led them to where Xisuturous,
With the Guidance of Belzebub,
Had Ridden Out the Deluge,
As had Noah.

Now Xisuturous and his wife
Had been Taken Immediately after the Flood,
By Ruse,
To Atla.

For Belzebub Feared for the Safety of Xisuturous, who was the main
    Symbol
Of Belzebub and Bael's Deceit of the Lord God.
And Belzebub Felt Atla was a safe Haven.
But his family was left where he had landed.

Then,
Because they were Told by Og,
And it was Confirmed by Ham's wife,
That Noah, Shem, Ham, Japeth and Canaan were Buried,

The Abandoned families of Noah
Married, Remarried and Multiplied
With the People
Of the Ship of Xisuturous.

And thus,
As Foretold by the Lord God,
The families of the sons of Noah and Heirs of Adam
Began to People the Earth with Spirit and Souls—

But Not as the Lord God had Expected.
And the Anger
Of the Lord God
Was Intense.

The Lord God Abandons Earth
Now the Deception of Noah by Og through Belzebub and Baal,
Agitated the Lord God to such a Degree,
That he Further Desired to Destroy the Earth of Beings.
But the Covenant of the Creator Prevented this Destruction,

But the Displeasure of the Lord was Extreme.
And the Lord God Left the Earth,
Vowing Never to Walk Upon its Ground Again.
And He Returned to the Kingdom of the Seventh Heaven.

Thus the Earth
Was Left Abandoned to Belzebub—
with his Adherence to Baal—
And the Tarnished Angels,

And a few Nephilim and Raphiem
Along with the Remnant of Mankind,
With a Scattering of Amen,
The Heirs of Noah and the Angels of God.

God, El,
Knew all Happenings on Earth.
But thus began
The great Confusion on Earth.

Belzebub and the Angels Rule the Earth
After the Lord God had Left the Earth
And the Deluge had Subsided,
The Tainted Angels Found the Land of Atla to be Crowded—
As did the Angels of God.

Then,
Because there were no longer any Restrictions by the Lord God,
They began again to Migrate
To other lands.

Now, as was the nature of Angels,
They Moved to the Cold of the high places of Earth,
And where the Sun
Would Come Upon their bodies.

They Built great Stone Dwellings,
Where the Streams and Pools were Purified of large amounts of Salt.
They Brought with them their Titanic sons, the Nephilim and Raphiem
And Gathered many Remnants of Man and Amen to Work for them.

But the great Conflict Remained on Atla
Where most Angels of God
And most Angels of Baal,
Stayed.

Now the Angels of Baal, now Known as sons of Baal,
Used the giant Nephilim and Raphiem
And those of Man that they brought to Atla as slaves
To work.

And Man was Treated in a Despicable Manner
To work the Mines
For Gold and Precious Stones and other Metals.
But the Angels of God Controlled the Crystals.

Now the Tarnished Angels though they Gave their Reverence to Baal,
Set themselves up as Gods.
And all those Beings that they Ruled were Forced to Worship them,
As well as Baal.

But the sons of God Worshiped only One God.
Now the sons of Baal Feared the sons of God and Left them alone.
But each of the Groups Attempted to Convert Beings
To their Way of Worship.

Then the Angels of Baal
Through their great Knowledge began again
To Experiment with the Ribbons of Life of Man and Animals
To Strengthen their Ability to Work.

As Time Passed they Changed the Threads of Life
Simply for their Venture and Pleasure.
And many Grotesque Creatures and Forms and Sizes
Came again Into Being.

And Souls Entering them became Confused.
Now those of Man who were the Heirs of Adam were with the Spirit of
    God
And Received Not the Ribbons of Life of Creatures
And they Remained Pure in Man's flesh and blood.

But those Offspring from Adam
Were few on Atla
And they became Wards
Of the Angels of God.

Now Og,
Who Brought Into the land of Babylon those families of Noah,
Became the Prolific Progenitor
Of great Tribes and Nations of Mighty Men and women.

His Offspring of Women
Became as Man Entered by Souls but Not Spirit,
Except those from the Heirs of Adam.
And Og did Not Die as did Man.

And Og Moved Ever Northward and then Eastward toward the land of
    Atla,
Fathering and Leading his huge families into Battles with others of Man
And also those Led by other Raphiem and Nephilim
For the sons of Baal.

And Og,
Who Teamed with his twin Brother, Sihon,
Feared No one or groups.
And great became the name of Og.[38]

Belzebub, who became Ruler of the Earth at the Departure of the Lord,
Reigned with Angels over all the Beings of Earth.
But Belzebub did Not Stay long on the land of Atla.
For he did Not Desire to be with the Angels of God.

With a few Corrupt Angels,
He Founded his own Colony
In the high places Above one of the larger Settlements
Formed by Og.

And Belzebub Renamed himself Belzeus,[39]
And Set himself Up
As the god of the Ogeans,
As they were Called after Og.

And all of the Ogeans Looked to the Tainted Angels as gods,
With Belzeus, the half Amphibian and half Archangel
As god
Of gods.

Now the Angels of God were great with Power and Knowledge.
And they Controlled the Crystals,
Which the sons of Baal
Had Not Discovered the Secret of their Making.

And though the sons of Baal
Feared the sons of God,
The Tainted Angels Still Caused Havoc and Confrontations
Among the other Beings of Earth.

Then the sons of God began to Move About the Earth
To Aid the poor Unfortunate Beings of Earth.
Now they Used the Power of the Crystals[40]
In their Transportation.

And they Took With them the Crystals
To their Major Kingships at three places
Upon the Lands where they Built great Pyramids
To Place the Crystals Atop Of.

The Amilous Comes to Earth
Now great was the Sorrow in the Heavens
And Glee in the Void
As the Earth
Had become more and more Corrupt.

But with the Movement of the Angels of God
Into the lands other than Atla,
Great became the Desire of the Amilous
To Save the Souls Upon the Earth.

And He Requested of the Almighty
That He might Come Upon the Earth in nature and Form of an Angel
To Assist the sons of God.
And Almighty, El, Agreed.

And the Amilous Came to Earth As Rael,
The Angel who Shown Like the Sun.
And He Came Into the land of Egypt, as the King
Affectionately Known as Ra.[41]

And Baal Knew.
And great became the Conflicts in the land of Egypt.
And many were the Atrocities
That were Performed by the Angels of Baal in the Name of Ra.

And
Great were the Lies
Told
In His Name.

Then the Angels of Baal Took Ra
And Placed Him in the great Pyramid of Egypt
Spread Him Upon a Slab and Filled His every Pore
With Salt.

And as Ra was Formed as an Angel,
His Body was No more
And His Spirit Returned to the Heavens
As the Amilous.

Now
All in the Heavens were Stunned,
For they Knew it was the Work of Baal, the Satan,
Through his Corrupted Angels.

Not Since the Disruption and Defection of Baal,
And the Deception of the Lord God
By the Serpent of Baal,
Through Adam and Eve,

Had there been such Shock and Dismay by the Almighty, El,
The Lord God, the Holy One,
The Amilous, himself,
And all the Beings in the Heavens.

And the Lord God Thought of Sending the Tarnished Angels
Into the Abyss Forever.
But the Great Spirit
Wished Not for Such a Victory for Baal.

Then the Almighty God Pronounced,
"I will Hold the Satan, Baal,
Within his Bounds of the Abyss
For One Thousand Years of the Earth.

And if the sons of Baal on the Earth
Are Not Redeemed to the Ways of God by then,
They will be Removed from Earth,
No longer may they Seek its Refuge."

Then began the Quest for Reformation for One Thousand Years,
And the great Power of the force was Used to Maintain the Heavens,
But Mainly as Intervention
Between the Heavens and the Void,

No New thing was Made
As the force Restrained Knowledge of or Action in
The Heavens and Earth from Baal
Or any of those Beings in the Chaos.

And many were the Converts by the sons of God and the Spirit of God.
But the Spirit within the elements of things,
As were the Angels, Nephilim, Raphiem and Man Made Of,
Did Not React as the Spirit did in the Heavens.

Now Belzebub,
Rankled by his Rejection as an Archangel by God,
Incited the sons of Baal and Man
To Deny the Will of God.

The Flight of the Angels
As the Thousand Years of the Binding of Baal to the Chaos
Came to its last One Hundred Years,
The sons of Baal became Fearful
Of the Wrath of God.

Now Belzebub Remembered the Words of God
That they would be Removed from Earth if they were Not Redeemed.
Then Belzebub Devised that the Angels of Baal and the Nephilim
Would Leave the Earth for another place in the Third Heaven.

And with the great Knowledge of Belzebub and the Angels of Baal,
They Scanned the nearest Planets that they could Live Upon.
And Belzebub Knew of a Mass with Water,
But Not within the Planets of the Sun.

But
It had its own Star.
And they Called it
(Sirius).

Then the Angels of Baal,
With their great Knowledge and Sight,
Began to Coordinate their Thoughts on Leaving the Earth
And Transporting themselves to (Sirius) with great Flying Craft.

And God
Made a Judgement Not to Intervene.
And Belzebub became Aware.
Then he Theorized the great Plan.

The Use of the Power of the Crystals was Paramount
And the Angels of God
Deemed they would Cooperate for their Purpose,
But only Under their Control.

Now the Angels Knew
Of the Power of the Alignment of Streams and great Rocks[42]
That would Allow them to Leave the Earth as they Circled it.
And the Alignment of the Rocks would Set the Course to (Sirius).

Most all on the Earth
Were Utilized to Build and Prepare
The Departure
Of the Angels of Baal.

And great was the Work of the Nephilim, Raphiem, Man and Amen,
Especially Upon Atla where the great Aircrafts were Constructed.
Then began Etched Records to Send Information and on Huge Stones
To Store the Knowledge of those that Worked Upon them.

Those who Mined and Forged the Metals
Or Aligned the Underground Streams
And Set the great Rocks and Built giant Statues of the Angels of Baal
Were Forced Into great Hardship.

Now some Six Thousand Years After the Deluge,
When Again for the most part,
The Beings on Earth, but those of the Angels of God and the Amen,
Were Filled with Corruption,

The Angels of Baal, Leaving Huge Formations to be Remembered,
Prepared to Leave the Earth
For their New Place, Far from Earth,
Led by Belzebub.

Now Belzebub and the Angels' Bodily nature
Was such
That they were mostly Impervious to the Cold
And Differences of the elements of the air.

But those Nephilim, those Raphiem and Man,
With the Vegetation and Seeds,
That the Angels of Baal were Taking with them,
Were to be Shielded.

Then before the Thousand Years were past
The sons of Baal,
With Belzebub,
Had Charted and Readied their Journey.

Their Vast Armada of Craft
Would Leave the Island of Atla from the Plains West of the City Atlantis
As the Sun's Rays Moved Along the Course of the four Crystals
Set About the Earth.

They would move Slowly Over the Crystal on Ba,
Set Atop the Pyramid on the high Mountain Peak to the West;
Then Angling North with Increasing Speed
Following the great Lines of Rocks and Underground Streams

In an Ever Tightening Circle of the Earth,
Then Angling South on the Final Course
Over the Pyramid Crystal
In the high Mountains of the East

And then on a straight Alignment
Over the Crystal
On Top the Pyramid on the Summit of the great Peak in Egypt
Where the Amilous had been Defiled with the Cross of Salt;

Then Over the Immense Crystal of Mount Atlas;
And finally High Over the Crystal of Ba to the West.
Ever Increasing in Height and Speed
On the Final Course,

Until the Armada Left the Earth
Over Ba,
Destined for their New Place—
As had the First of the Group.

The Sons of Baal and Belzebub Leave Earth—But Baal Enacts Revenge
On the morning
That Ended the Thousand Years of Bondage of Baal
From the Knowledge of the Heavens,
The great Armada Rose En masse from the Vast Plains of Atla

Just as the First Rays of the Sun Hit the Crystals on Atlas
Focusing its Immense Power
To the Aircrafts of Belzebub and the sons of Baal.
And their Voyage Began.

Now the Spirit of the Amilous, after His Cross of Salt Disintegration,
Had Transposed to the Heavens from the Pyramid of Egypt
At Dawn, and the Beginning of the Thousand Year Intervention
Of Baal's Awareness of the Heavens, were Simultaneous.

And by the Time the Sun Rays Arrived on the Crystals
Of the Pyramid of Mount Atlas at the End of Baal's Banishment,
The Satan had Already Knowledge
Of the Evacuation of Belzebub and the Angels of Baal from the Earth.

And it was as the Lord God Wished, for it was to be Baal's Humiliation
That his First Perception of the Heavens and Earth
In One Thousand Years,
To Find of the Banishment of those who Worshiped Him.

But the Lord God
Had Not Judged the Keen Shrewdness of Baal
And his Development in the Abyss
During the One Thousand Years.

By the Time the Armada was on their Last Course
For Leaving the Earth
Baal was well Aware
Of all that was Happening.

Then as Belzebub and the sons of Baal
Moved Away from the Earth onto their Journey,
Baal with his Knowledge and Use of the force,
Controlled the Crystals.

And the Beams from the Sun
Were then at such an Angle,
And as Baal Directed the Crystals,
That the Energy Transmitted was Intense.

The three Crystals of Egypt, Atlas and Ba were Aligned
To Give a Thrust Power to the Armada,
But this Harmony of Light Intensified Into a Thermal Power,
For a Brief Time—greater than the Light of the Sun.

And the Earth was Scorched
By the Radiation of Light
From the Pyramid in Egypt to the West
Through Atla and to Ea.

But the Focus of the Sun
Came Upon the Crystals of Atla
And the Intensity of the Energy Broke Open
The Bowels of the Earth Under Atla and Ba.

The Violence of the Energy of the Light
Disintegrated the Crystals of Egypt and Atla.
The Crystals of Ba were Absorbed Into the Depths of the Seas
As Ba was Fragmented and mostly Sank Into the Seas.

The Turbulence of the Earth Underneath Atla
Erupted with such Violence
That Atla was Broken Wholly Apart
And it Totally Descended Into the Seas.[43]

Then the land Beneath the great Elevation,
Upon which the Pyramid and Statue Rested in Egypt,
Settled
To the Level of the Seas.[44]

There was Total Demolishment
Of the lands of Atla,
A Breaking Up of Ba[45]
A Changing to a Valley of the Nile in Egypt,[46]

There was a Scorching of the Earth
From the Pyramid of Egypt to the West
And the Lush Gardens of Vegetation
Were No More.[47]

By the Time the Sun had Passed Over the Opposite Side of Ba,
The First Day of the Release of Satan's Knowledge Into the Heavens,
The Destruction by the Crystals
Was Done.

But there Remained the giant Tidal Waves
That Rolled Over the many lands of Earth
And Darkening Debris in the heaven of Earth
Over the Cataclysm.

Then God,
But for the Angel Kings,
Brought all the Angels of God on Earth
As Spirits Once more Into the Heavens

Now Baal Knew of the Anger of God,
And he Restrained himself from Further Actions
In the Heavens and on the Earth.
And God Knew and Waited.

Then Man,
The Remnants of Amen, with their Angel Kings,
Again Inherited the Earth—
In its Confusion from the Incendiary, Darkness and Floods,

Then the Lord God Remembered Noah and his sons,
And He Ordered Og to Free them from the Caves of Baal.
And Og Brought them Out, following Six Thousand Years Suspension,
But Og Lay Noah Naked in an Open Tent for all to see.[48]

And, as Recorded,
When they Awoke Ham was Contemptuous of his Father, Noah,
For his Drunkenness
And Ridiculed him.

Then Noah Learning of his Stupor and also his sons—
Though Not its length—
Remembered Ham's son Canaan had Given him the drink.
And Noah Cursed Canaan to be a Servant to his brothers forever.

But Noah was old and Knew Not Ever
That it was the Sinking of Atla and much of Ba
That Caused the Floods that were About him
And Not the Ones of Old.

And Noah Found Out Not
Of the Abandonment
Of the Lord God
Of the Earth,

And Not the Turmoil
Caused by Belzebub and the Fallen Angels of Baal
For Six Thousand Years
Or their Flight from Earth.

Nor did Shem,
Who became the Spokesman
After Noah.
For God Intervened,

Causing a Dream-like State in the Minds
Controlled by Souls,
But Not Noah's sons or Noah,
Who had been Suspended for over Six Thousand Years.

And it Lasted for the Life of Noah
Who Recalled the Deluge and Before.
Others Remembered as a Dream, the Time of Belzebub's Control of Earth,
As did their Offspring.

But, Ham, Stepfather of Og, Followed Og into the lands of Babylon,
Ham Slowly Uncovered the Concealment Duping of Noah and his sons—
And their families' Desertion of them,
Through the questioning of Og.

And Ham Deduced
The Forsaking by the Lord God of Earth to the Corrupt Angels.
And again, there were Floods and Tales of great Moving Disturbances
About the Earth with clouds Causing Dark of Night.

And Ham was Contemptuous of the Lord God
And he Set Out
To Build a Ziggurat Tower so High
That the Lord God Could Not Submerge it.[49]

And it would Rise Above the Cloud Debris
That Moved About the Earth.
And he Prepared
To Gather all the Heirs of Adam and Eve About him.

Now it Displeased the Lord God to be Treated with such Disrespect
And He Knew Ham's Effort
Would Stop the Spreading of the Spirit of God
And Living Souls to all of Man.

Then the Lord God
Confounded the Language of the Heirs of Noah
And they Scattered Upon the face of the Earth.
And the Anger of the Lord God was Recorded by Shem.

Now long had been the Confinement of the Remnants of Original Man
In Pockets About the lands of Earth.
And the Uniqueness of their Features had Developed
Within the Kingdoms and Tribes of Man.

But the Multitude of the Corruptions of Man and Beasts
Had been Destroyed in the Cataclysm Caused by the Crystals and Baal.
Now the Entry of the Heirs of Adam and Noah
Spread Across the Earth.

Thus the Renewal of Man and the Cleansing of the Souls
Was the grand Undertaking on the Earth.
But the sons of Noah, themselves,
Did Not Leave their lands.

And
At the End of the Time of Noah,
When the Illusions of the Minds of Souls
Was Released,

The Lord God Sent The Metatron, Sandalphon (the Dark Earthly Female
     Angel)
And the Trusted Archangels,
To Aid the Angel Kings for a Period of Time—
And God Involved the Amilous.

I, The Metatron, have Come Here with the Sandalphon to Guide those
Who were Separated by the Sinking of Atla.
I am The Metatron and I am the Recorder of God
And Will be Known by Many Names.

Remember—Vanity in the Soul is the Evil that Intensifies all Evils.

Notes

Introduction

1 (page 8). The white man-god was known and spoken about by almost all American Indian tribes. When Cortez (the Spaniard who conquered the Aztecs) arrived in Central America, he was thought to be the returning white man-god, who was revered by the Aztecs for centuries

2 (page 8). Throughout the northern part of South America, Central America, and the southern part of North America, giant stone structures, especially pyramids, have been found that rivaled or eclipsed those in Egypt. Present-day engineers marvel at how they were made. Archaeological discoveries show amazing methods of irrigation and food production in the past in this part of the world. These Indians were also far advanced in astronomical knowledge. Up to this time, archaeologists have been at a loss to explain this phenomenal ability on the part of what they believe was an otherwise primitive culture.

3 (page 8). Archeologists were amazed at the seemingly barbaric practices of Indian tribes such as the Aztecs, who cut out the hearts of slaves and possibly some of their own. The statues of the great plumed serpents adorn some of the walls of the enormous stone structures. The

plumed serpent was also called Quetzalcoatl, as was the white man-god. Was this the fallen Archangel Belzebub who came to destroy the works of the real Quetzacoatl—The Metatron? Whole Indian civilizations abandoned their great sites almost overnight in some places. Was this caused by Belzebub?

Revelations of The Metatron

4 (page 45). A fable by an Indian tribe in what is now Peru tells of the white man-god and his dark twin sister being born as adults to an Indian mother after she had swallowed an emerald. Were these the appearance of The Metatron and Sandalphon? Did the Sandalphon go to the Middle East and Africa and become the Queen of Sheba? Writings, including the Bible (see I Kings, chapter 10) tell of the fabulously wealthy Queen of Sheba's visit to the great King Solomon. She brought him overwhelmingly expensive gifts, including vast amounts of gold. She was originally portrayed as dark-skinned and extremely statuesque. Only religious artists in later years show her as light-skinned. The Bible says Solomon gave the Queen of Sheba everything she desired. Did this include a child by him? Was the Old Testament dialogue *Song of Solomon* written by or for them? The great emperor of Ethiopia, Haile Selassie, claimed he was a direct descendant of their union. Ethiopians to this day claim the Ark of the Covenant of God is hidden and guarded in Ethiopia.

5 (page 48). Though the mind of God is expected, the Eye of God has been brought down from ancient times by many groups—especially Egypt and the Masons. The United States dollar bill has an eye on a pyramid.

6 (page 48). The basic unit of all matter is still to be discovered by scientists.

7 (page 53). Many religions believe in a Trinity of God—gods.

8 (page 53). This may explain the Trinity of Great Spirits with one God still supreme.

9 (page 55). The name Amilous or similar names appear in numerous references to a Holy Being—a son of God. Edgar Cayce, the sleeping prophet, mentions a similar name in his readings while under hypnosis.

10 (page 56). I AM has been frequently mentioned in relationship to God. In Jewish history I AM and God are as one.

11 (page 56). THE WORD is given much attention in the Christian New Bible in John, chapters 1–14.

12 (page 58). The Metatron is mentioned in many ancient and modern writings about angels. He was known as the First Angel and Scribe of God. The Metatron is also known by many other names.

13 (page 58). The Sandalphon is mentioned in writings as the twin of The Metatron. The Sandalphon was known by many other names.

14 (page 59). Though much has been written about angels, their names and the order of angels varies widely. However, the writers seem to have had an inherent knowledge of angels and their Orders.

15 (page 63). Perhaps this is why it is said that each soul in human has a guardian angel.

16 (page 65). As most have proclaimed, the soul is free willed.

17 (page 67). Archangels are sometimes referred to as angels, but this portrays them as somewhat different.

18 (page 71). Many writers have written of the Akashic records, or the Book of Life.

19 (page 73). Was this the "Big Bang" to which scientists refer?

20 (page 84). The following description of the basic formation and evolution of life on earth does not conflict with theories of a multitude of scientists.

21 (page 91). Scientists have recently reluctantly concluded after years of extensive research in the most barren of places, including the Antarctica, that organisms cannot have a life without some form of water. Some organisms may stay in a dormant state for thousands of years and then come to life with the introduction of some form of water.

22 (page 129). Perhaps these were those known as the Neanderthal men and women.

23 (page 133). Present-day scientists overwhelmingly say that the lands of earth were almost all one mass millions of years ago. They refer to it as Pangea. Pangea was separated into the present continental

formations through cataclysmic upheavals as well as slowly drifting apart. Various theories exist as to the separations.

24 (page 138). Was this the beginning of what are now known as black holes? A super-massive black hole has been reported to have been discovered. It is thought to be the size of a billion solar masses.

25 (page 139). Was this one of those times that scientists record as an ice age, or was this more severe than that?

26 (page 140). Was this the first Hebrew Biblical account of Creation in Genesis? There appears to be a separation of the first chapter plus the first and second verses of Genesis and the rest of the second chapter. The Metatron's version eventually seems to fill this in.

27 (page 143). The *Discover* Magazine article, "Moon of our Delight" (Jan. 1993 page 72), declares that our large moon keeps the Earth from spinning wildly. This stabilization plus the tilt of the Earth gives us our seasons.

28 (page 144). Were these the Cro-Magnon humans? This would possibly account for the scientific claims that *Homo sapiens* is 30–100,000 years old or older.

29 (page 153). This would appear to be the time that is known as the fall of a third of the Angels and the beginning of the great divide between God and Satan the Devil.

30 (page 157). Was this the fabled Atlantis?

31 (page 161). This may be the account of the second chapter of Genesis.

32 (page 163). Benjamin Walker, in his book *Man and the Beast Within* (Stein and Day), notes that contrasting that which is not material in mankind can be reduced to three main groups: (1) The senses of the physical body, (2) intellectual mind, and (3) spiritual-mind-driven functions in Man. He finds this belief of the three separations in such diverse groups as ancient Egyptian, Babylonian, Chinese, Japanese, Zoroastrian, Tibetan (Bon), Hindu, Voodoo, Greek (Aristotle), Greek (Plutarch), Jewish, Moslem, and medieval Church scholastics. (Also numerous other religions and psychiatric groups similar separation of mind. or an interesting review see Walker's book.)

33 (page 170). Refer to Genesis 5:21–24. 21. When Enoch was sixty five years he fathered Methuselah. 22. Enoch walked with God; and lived three hundred years after the birth of Methuselah and fathered sons and daughters. 23. And in all the days of Enoch were three hundred sixty-five years. 24. And he walked with God, and was seen no more: because God took him.

34 (page 171). Refer to Genesis 6:1–4: 1. When people began to multiply upon the Earth, and daughters were born to them, 2. the sons of God saw the daughters of men were fair and took them as wives of all which they chose.... 4. Nephilim were upon the earth in those days—and afterward—and the sons of God after going into the daughters of men brought forth children, these were the mighty men of old, men of renown.

35 (page 174). Refer to Genesis 6:5–22 and chapters 7 and 8: 6. God repented he had made Man on Earth.... 7. He said "I will destroy him"—and the beasts"—8. But Noah found favor with the Lord.

36 (page 176). Xisuturous was mentioned in the writings of Gilgamesh the great Sumerian King. Xisuturous was also translated from other writings as Ziusudra or Utnpishtim, as well as other names.

37 (page 179). It is possible that Og, (King Og, one of the last of the Rephaim—see Joshua 12:4) was one of the most important beings from the time of the Great Flood until his defeat and probable killing by Moses—with the help of God. (See Numbers 21: 33–35.) He lived an amazingly long life of thousands of years. Though Og was very important in Jewish written history, only his defeat was recorded in the Torah. It also may be true that Og traveled extensively outside the Middle East and was vitally important in what is now the Agean, Western Asia, all of Europe, and the British Isles until his return to the Middle East and his death.

An extensive biography of Og can be found in the *Encyclopaedia Judacia* (Jerusalem: Keter Publishing House, 1978). They confirm Og was a very important being in Jewish history. Og and his brother Sihon (also mentioned in the Old Testament) were born to the wife of Ham (Noah's son) by Ahijah, who was the son of the fallen Angel Shambazai before the Great Deluge. The Old Testament mentions their great size as giants among men.

38 (page 185). Further reference to Og: There are legends from all over the Agean, Europe, including the Scandinavian countries, the British Isles, and Western Asia about a giant that appeared and led their tribes in ancient times.

For example:

ODIN—Scandinavian

WODAN—Germanic

GUNGINAR— Norse

DONAR—Anglo-Saxon

TWIN GODS—Anglo-Saxon, worshipped along the North Sea

GOG AND MAGOG—British Isles

An Oak Tree was also revered in the Germanic part of Europe, and its destruction was a major victory for the invaders.

OGHAMA—Celts; the Gault divinity Ogmios had his name subverted by the Gallo-Romans. (From the *Encyclopedia of Religion*, bk. 11 (New York: MacMillian Publishing Company, 1987)

39 (page 185). Belzeus, shortened to Zeus, was the well known god of the Greeks before and at the time of Jesus and mentioned in the New Testament in Acts 14:12.

40 (page 186). Atlantis legends are rife with crystal power.

41 (page 186). Many tales were written about Ra, who shone like the sun—also about his atrocities.

42 (page 190). Throughout the middle part of earth, north and south of the equator, a multitude of unexplained, ancient, purposely built, immense rock formations have been found. Besides such structures, long lines and clusters of placed boulders have been discovered in the same areas of the world. Could these have been used by the fallen Angels for power in abandoning earth? Many formations are also aligned for astronomical purposes—such as Stonehenge.

43 (page 194). Much has been written and told about the destruction of Atlantis.

44 (page 194). Though Khufu (Cheops), the Egyptian Pharaoh, claimed to have built the Great Pyramid, his work has been disputed by many Egyptologists. They say his work was only to refurbish the worn outside of the Great Pyramid and the Sphinx beside it. The noted author, Zecharia Sitchin, in his article, "The Great Pyramid Forgery" in *Fate* magazine, July 1993, expands on this, saying the

Great Pyramid was many thousand years old when Khufu (Cheops) became Pharaoh in Egypt.

45 (page 194). Submerged, giant, road-like rock formations have been found off the coast of Florida into the Bahamas. The so-called Devil's Triangle is also in this area.

46 (page 194). The article, "The Mud That Was Egypt," in *Discover* magazine (Jan. 1993, p. 81) reveals that latest research finds that the mud of the Nile Delta did not appear until at least 6500 B.C. Before that it was sand.

47 (page 194). Scientists say the deserts of the west of Egypt—the Eastern Desert, Nubian Desert, Lybian Desert, and Sahara Desert—were once lush areas of plant life. The finding in these deserts of glass which was formed by intense heat has been a mystery to scientists. The Sahara Desert is mostly a hard, rocky surface with only a small part of sand.

48 (page 195). Reference to this is in Genesis 9:18–27: 18. The sons of Noah who came out of the ark were Shem, Ham and Japheth. And Ham was the father of Canaan. 19. These three were the sons of Noah and from these all mankind spread over the whole earth. 20. Now Noah was a farmer and began to till the soil and planted himself a vineyard. 21. He drank wine and became drunk and lay uncovered in his tent. 22. And Ham, the father of Canaan, saw his father was naked and told his two brothers who were outside. 23. Then Shem and Japheth put a cloak upon their shoulders, and going backward covered their father's nakedness. 24. When Noah awakened from the wine and when he learned what his younger son had done to him. 25 he said: Cursed be Canaan: a servant to servants shall he be unto his brethren. 26 Then he said: Blessed be the Lord God of Shem and let Cannan be his servant. 27 May God enlarge Jepheth, and may he dwell in the tents of Shem; and may Canaan be his servant. 28 And Noah lived another three hundred fifty years after the flood.

Editor's note: Was Canaan actually Og? In other Jewish writings, Og was to be the servant of Noah and his family forever. If the writings of The Metatron are not true, why is this event such a major happening? Why is a man (Noah) alone in his tent naked such a catastrophe? He was drunk and he blamed Canaan for that? Why? The Metatron explains.

49 (page 197). The Tower of Babel was another great occurrence that is
further explained by The Metatron's writings. For reference to this
event, see Genesis 10:32 and 11:1–9.

Editor's final notes: (1) Was the Lord God (See Revelations, page
53) the one called Yahweh or Jehovah by the ancient Hebrews? (2)
Many countries surrounding the Hebrew tribes in the time of Moses
worshiped a fish-tailed god. Was this actually Belzebub? (3) Below is a
more complete history of Og and Sihon taken from the *Encyclopaedia
Judacia* (Jerusalem, Kettering Publishing House, 1978), pages 1341 and
1342.

OG (Heb. עוֹג, עֹג). ruler of Bashan, one of the Amorite kings in the
Transjordan area during the time of Moses. The Bible remembers
Og as belonging to the race of giants "who was left of the remaining Rephaim," and special attention is paid to the description of his
huge iron bedstead (Deut. 3:11). The Kingdom of Og comprised
Bashan and the Hermon region, and extended to the Jordan river
to the west (Josh. 12:4-5). Three or four of the cities of his kingdom
are mentioned in the Bible: Ashtaroth, which was apparently his
capital and known as the capital of the realm (Tell el-Amarna let-
ters, no. 197, possibly also Karnaim, cf. Gen. 14:5); Salcah (Josh 12:5;
13:11, et al.); and Edrei (Num. 21:33; Josh 13:12, 31). From this it
would appear that his kingdom was one of the remaining Hyksos
kingdoms whose cities at that time were scattered in Palestine. It
is also posible that this kingdom was established by Amerites who
invaded the area in the time of the Egyptian-Hittite struggle during the Reign of Rameses II (13th century). Og was defeated by the
Israelites when the eastern side of the Jordan was conquered by
those who left Egypt (Num. 21:33, 35; Deut. 3:1ff.) Half of the tribe
of Manasseh took Og's land as their inheritance (Josh. 13:31). This
victory greatly strengthened the spirit of the people. "Sixty towns
...fortified with high walls, gates, and pillars" were then conquered (Deut. 3:4,5). Echoes of this victory, which was of excep-
tional importance, are also encountered in later passages (Josh.
13:12; Ps. 135:11; 136:20; Neh. 9:22).   [Jo.S.]

Og and Sihon in the Aggadah. Sihon and Og were the sons of
Ahijah, whose father was the fallen angel Shamḥazai (Nid. 61a),
and of Ham's wife (Yal. Reub. on Gen. 7:7). Og was born before the
Flood and was saved from it by Noah on the promise that he and
his descendants would serve Noah as slaves in perpetuity (PdRE

23). Sihon and Og were giants, their foot alone measuring 18 cubits (Deut. R. 1:25). Og is identified with Eliezer, the servant of Abraham, who received him as a gift from Nimrod. So that he could not claim reward in the world to come for his services to his master, God paid him in this world by making him a king (Sof. 21:9; ed. M. Higger (1937) 366 and PdRE 16). During his reign he founded 60 cities, which he surrounded with high walls, the lowest of which was not less than 60 miles in height (Sof. *ibid.*). When Og, who was present at the feast Abraham made on the occasion of Isaac's weaning, was teased by all the great men assembled there for having called Abraham a sterile mule, he pointed contemptuously at Isaac, saying, "I can crush him by putting my finger on him," whereupon God said to him, "Thou makest mock of the gift given to Abraham—by thy life thou shalt look upon myriads of his descendants, and thy fate shall be to fall into their hands" (Gen. R. 53:10). Sihon, appointed by the other kings as guardian of Erez Israel, extracted tribute from them (Num. R. 19:29). Sihon and Og were even greater enemies of Israel than was Pharaoh (Mid. Ps. 136:11). When Moses was about to attack them, God assured him that he had nothing to fear, for He had put their guardian angels in chains (*ibid.* and Deut. R. 1:22). Though Moses was undaunted by Sihon, he did fear Og, because he had been circumcised by Abraham (Zohar, Num. 184a) and because of the possibility that the latter's merit might stand him in good stead for having been the "one who escaped and told Abraham" (Gen. 11:13; Nid. 61a). Moses' fears were unfounded, however, in that Og's real motive had been to bring about the death of Abraham so that he could marry Sarah (Deut. R. 1:25).

Sihon was left to his own resources by Og, who was confident of his brother's ability to conquer Israel unaided (Song R. 4:8). Og himself met his death when a mountain three parasangs long, which he had uprooted to cast upon the camp of Israel, was invaded by ants dispatched by God as he carried it upon his head toward his destination. The perforated mountain slipped from Og's head to his neck, whereupon Moses struck him upon the ankle with an ax and killed him (Ber. 54a b). Though the victory over Sihon and Og was as important as the crossing of the Red Sea, Israel did not sing a song of praise to God upon it as they had upon Pharaoh's destruction, the omission not being made good until the time of David (Mid. Ps. 136:11).   [ED.]

Bibliography: Aharoni, Land, 191; Noth, Hist. Isr, 159 60; idem, in: BBLA, 1 (1949), 1ff.: Bergman (Biran), in JPOS, 16 (1936), 224 54; Y. Kaufmann, *Sefer Yehoshu'a* (1959), 166, IN THE AGGADAH: Ginzberg, Legends, index.

To order additional copies of this book,
please send full amount plus $4.00 for
postage and handling for the first book and
50¢ for each additional book.

Send orders to:

Galde Press, Inc.
PO Box 460
Lakeville, Minnesota 55044-0460

Credit card orders call 1–800–777–3454
Phone (612) 891–5991 • Fax (612) 891–6091
Visit our website at http://www.galdepress.com

Write for our free catalog.